THE MOVE

FROM THE SHALLOWS
INTO THE DEEP

PHILLIP BAKER

Judy,
go deep!
PBaker

AMERICA'S PRESS
LEAGUE CITY, TEXAS

Phillip Baker Ministries
P.O. Box 1708
Dickinson, Texas 77539
www.phillipbaker.org

Scripture marked (KJV) are taken from *The Holy Bible* King James Version. Accessed on Bible Gateway. www.BibleGateway.com

Scripture marked (NIV) are taken from *The Holy Bible*, New International Version. Accessed on Bible Gateway. www.BibleGateway.com

ZONDERVAN PUBLISHING HOUSE. Scripture marked (AMP) are taken from *The Amplified New Testament*. Copyright 1958 by the Lockman Foundation.

Book Layout ©2017 BookDesignTemplates.com

The Move - From the Shallows into the Deep/Phillip Baker. —1st ed.
ISBN 978-0-692-97284-7

ENDORSEMENTS

"It has been my privilege for several years to have known and traveled with Phillip Baker to Pacific Island countries such as Papua New Guinea, Solomon Islands, Vanuatu, and to my homeland, Australia. His balanced ministry has been accepted whether we have been teaching national pastors, college students, or church congregations. Irrespective of whatever culture Phillip encountered, he was able to adapt and make a positive and lasting impact for the Kingdom of God. Phillip Baker has become a special friend to Irene and myself over the years we have known each other."

Missionary, Dr. Graham Baker
Papua New Guinea and The World

"For several years, I have known Phillip Baker. I have witnessed his heart for the people when we ministered together in Tanzania, Africa. Brother Phillip is serious about building God's Kingdom and raising up God's Leaders. It is not just empty words for Phillip Baker, because he is leading by example in his personal life, along with his powerful wife Laura, to raise up their three wonderful children.

When you are with Phillip you are showered by love, God's Love, and you do not want to leave. The Presence of God is real in Brother Phillip's life and ministry, and he brings blessings to the people around him. It is always a great pleasure and honor when Brother Phillip comes to Tanzania, and I trust that you will feel the same about his ministry after reading this book."

Missionary, Dr. Egon Falk
New Life Outreach
Tanzania and The World

"Thank you for being such a loyal friend and brother in Christ. Having served as The Pastor of a local church for over 40 years, I have been aware of your importance as "the exposer" of the fivefold ministry. Since 2003, you have shown yourself to be approved as one of God's Evangelists to The Church."

Emeritus Pastor, Robert Dowdy
Church of the Living God
Galveston, Texas

"My wife and I have been privileged to be close friends with Phillip and Laura Baker since 1994. I know of no other Evangelist with a greater passion to seeThe Local Church thrive and operate in the fullness of God's calling and blessing. Our church has been deeply impacted by Phillip Baker Ministries, and I am confident that the wisdom of God will be imparted to you through The Move. Furthermore, I believe that as you read The Move you will be strengthened and enriched in your daily walk with Jesus."

Pastor John Gilligan
Living Faith Outreach
Dickinson, Texas

DEDICATIONS

I have always believed that relationships build The Kingdom. It is a principle in which I have built my entire life and ministry. I can, without a doubt, tell you that relationships have built me and made this book possible!

Thank you:

The person who has believed in me more than any other, is my wife! The Father knew I was going to need a great deal of help in order to do everything He called me to do, so, He gave me Laura. There is no PBM or *The Move* without her! Love you more!

Keegan, Madisen, and McKinley, you were so in my heart as I wrote this book. With everything in me, I want you to live and enjoy God's Will for your life. I love you guys, and ultimately, this book belongs to you and is for you more than any other.

Lonell and Bonnie Smith, my grandparents, who picked me up every Sunday morning and took me to church. That is where my love for The Local Church was fostered. My Grandma Bonnie was filled with the Holy Spirit and prayed us all into The Deep. I wouldn't have been introduced to The Deep without her.

My Mom and Dad, Johnny and Glenda Baker who gave me a freedom when I was growing up to become very independent and to grow in my own relationship with Jesus. I will be forever grateful for this gift.

Throughout my life, God has strategically placed many great men and women of God, Pastors, and ministry gifts that have molded and impacted my life. You believed in me, sowed The Word into my heart, and prayed for me. I know without you, I could not be the person I am today.

To all of the churches, businesses, and people that Monthly Partner with PBM! You all are miracles in our life. We have been able to go to churches regardless of their size, never preach with a check in mind, and go to the nations with the Gospel because of YOU! Everywhere we go, you go. We will be forever grateful to you for believing in us!

Finally, it's all about Jesus! Growing up, the only thing in which I ever believed I was good at, was knowing HIM! The only thing I have ever wanted to do was preach about HIM. Thank you Jesus for giving me the honor of representing you throughout the world, your Churches, and ultimately my life!

ACKNOWLEDGEMENTS

To the team that helped make *The Move* a reality! Thank you Savanna Rojas for pouring through the book with your editing skills and giving my words more polish. Lorena Garza for your creativity in the design of the book cover. Charity Emmite for all your photography skills, connecting *The Move* and Phillip Baker Ministries with social media and helping us maximize the release of the book. And my incredible wife, Laura, who brought everything together at the end of the process. I am forever grateful for all of your hard work.

CONTENTS

FORWARD

I was honored to be asked to write the forward for *The Move*. I have known Phillip since he was 12 years old, and I can describe him in one word – different. As a child, he would get himself up (even when his parents did not attend church), get himself ready, and make sure that his grandparents would come by to take him to church. Then as a teenager, Phillip never fell into the sinful traps or made the big mistakes that others typically make in their teen years. Additionally, when Phillip was a young adult he made good choices, such as choosing Laura to be his forever partner. Phillip and Laura have three wonderful children (Keegan, Madisen, and McKinley) on whom rests the distinctive mark of being raised in a Godly home by Godly parents. Phillip and Laura are different, and I mean that in every good way. Laura runs the home, while Philip travels, and she is the perfect complement to Phillip. Laura is an excellent wife, mother, and an exceptional minister of the Gospel of Jesus Christ. Phillip and Laura served alongside me, as my youth and children's pastors, before going to work at Texas Bible Institute for Tommy and Rachel Burchfield. In every station of life, Phillip and Laura have proven themselves to be faithful and fruitful.

Interestingly, Phillip and I love sports! We often talk about "pound for pound" who is the greatest fighter in the world. Phillip, to me, is a man who will "pound for pound" lift your church to greater heights. The greatest ministers typically do one thing exceptionally well, such as: teach, love people, organize, or flow in The Spirit. Did you notice the word "or?" Phillip's abilities to teach on leadership, finance, marriage, and then flow in the healing anointing, make him the "total package!" He is a quadruple threat to the devil, and a great blessing to any church or ministry.

Phillip has added writing to his extensive resume, with the completion of *The Move*. Personally, I enjoyed this book very much and I can assure you, dear reader; *The Move* will keep you moving forward in all things concerning your life and the Kingdom of God. Phillip sees things differently. He also says things differently. I love Phillip Baker, because he is different.

Paul Troquille
Leadership Training International
Bossier City, Louisiana

INTRODUCTION

"DEEP CALLETH UNTO DEEP..."
PSALM 42:2 KJV

These are the very first words, and the very first
scripture that I want you to see as you begin to read *THE
MOVE!* "Why?" you might ask. Well, this scripture is at the
core of everything I am about, everything a believer should
be about, and everything this book is about. The deep in
the heart of The Father is calling out to the deep in us! The
questions are, "Do we hear it?" and "Do we want to hear
it?" When I meditate on Psalm 42:2, I cannot help but realize that where there is deep, there is also shallow. Ever
since I was a teenager, my desire has been to be deep, but
greater still has been my desire *not* to be shallow. This
strong desire came from what I was observing in life.
Growing up, I saw shallow everywhere! I saw shallow in
my schools, in my church, and I watched shallow people
do what they always do, which is to hurt others out of their
own emotional and spiritual immaturity. Being in full-time
ministry since 1990, I have continued to see people re-
peatedly hurt themselves, hurt others, and hurt The Kingdom of God because of their immaturity, selfishness, and
pride. What about you? Do you see shallow in the world?

Have you known some shallow believers? Have you been in some shallow churches? The answers to many of these questions may be "yes;" but there is still one question that very few people want to ask themselves, and that is, "Have *I* been a bit shallow myself?" It is time to admit that it is easier to spot "shallow" in others, than it is to recognize "shallow" in ourselves. There are very few people who possess the maturity necessary to step outside themselves, and be objective. Most of the time, we as people, rather than owning our shallowness, simply justify and minimize our actions and words. As the old saying goes, "We judge others by their actions, but we want others to judge us by our intentions." How about I define "shallow" a little bit more? What does being shallow mean? So that we are all on the same page, here are some thoughts to get us started.

Believers tend to be captives, instead of deliverers!

Of course, your first goal is to be set free. It is never God's best for you to be in bondage. Having established that truth in our lives, the goal should quickly shift from celebrating our own freedom; to actively helping others be set free by using the power we received at the New Birth. God sets you free because He loves you; but also, because you can then in turn, lead others to the same glorious freedom you have experienced. Can you guess what all the great heroes of the Bible have in common? They were deliverers! We are also called to be deliverers in The Kingdom of God, in the world, and in His Churches. The very last thing we want to do is spend our life needing to be delivered. We do not want darkness to consume us. Our goal should be to walk boldly into the darkness, and guide people out into the light. One more time, you are called to be a deliverer, and deliverers, deliver!

Believers tend to be customers, not servants!

People typically walk into churches in the same manner with which they walk into restaurants. They go into "critique mode!" *"I like this, but I do not like that. I would like a booth, not a table. It is too bright, or it is too dark. There are too many items on the menu, or there are not enough items on the menu. I like the music, or I do not like the music. The waitress does not check on us enough, or the waitress checks on us too much."* Every minute in a restaurant these thoughts are running through our minds, and most of the time this occurs without our consent. We have been trained to think this way, because we have been taught *"the customer is always right."* This "customer mentality" is fine for a restaurant, but that spirit does not belong in church. We are supposed to be servants in The Kingdom of God, in the world, and in His Churches. Jesus had a servant's heart, the Disciples had a servant's heart, the early church had a servant's heart, the Apostle Paul had a servant's heart, everyone in Heaven has a servant's heart, angels have a servant's heart, and WE also should have a servant's heart. What do servants do? They serve!

Believers tend to be watchers, instead of worshippers!

People think they are worshippers because they go to church, and that worship is something you do only at church. These same people believe they are worshippers because their church plays slow songs. Many people think that worship is reserved for those that sing well or play an instrument. Simply put, worship is the expression of your love for God. Worship is expressing that love, not watching what may be happening around you, until it is time to sit down. Worship is not only about telling Jesus you love Him, but SHOWING Him! I love the saying, "An inward experience has an outward manifestation." In the Bible, worship was expressed using their body, for example, shouting, singing, bowing, dancing, clapping, lifting their hands and so much more. We are to be worshippers in The Kingdom of God, in the world, and in His Churches. Remember, worshippers worship!

Believers tend to be offended, instead of forgiving!

There are many believers in churches today who are just one negative experience away from being offended to the point, that they would walk away from who God has called them to be, and away from what God has called them to do! And I promise you that the enemy is working hard to make sure you have ample opportunity to be offended. It is one of his greatest weapons to use on believers. How many people in your city are not in church, not building the Kingdom of God, because they were offended? Our cities are filled with bitter people, who are on the sidelines of The Kingdom of God, instead of pursuing their incredible potential and fulfilling their Kingdom Assignment. These people are offended, and they cannot, or they choose not to forgive. I am unsure of who said it first, but I took the following quote to heart years ago; "Bitterness is me drinking poison and hoping the other person dies." Please understand that I am not minimizing what may have happened to you. No doubt it was horrible and unthinkable and at the very least, just mean and uncaring, but regardless of the offense, you *must* choose to forgive for your own sake. Truly, offense may be the greatest weapon ever formed against believers. Every believer must realize that they will have a tremendous amount of opportunities to be offended, if they purpose themselves to build The Kingdom of God. Believers must choose to forgive, *when*, not *if* it happens. Remember, forgivers forgive!

> ***Captives, customers, watchers,***
> ***and the offended are SHALLOW.***
> ***I wrote this book for all those who***
> ***pray for less of SHALLOW***
> ***and more of DEEP in their***
> ***lives! Is that you? It is most***
> ***definitely what I desire!***

Let us look at the deep and shallow thought processes from a different perspective. Over the years I have urged people numerous times to be deep, and not shallow. I have challenged people through the following analogies:

be a river and not a puddle, be fire and not smoke, be an eagle and not a parrot, be a voice to your generation and not just an echo. Have I made my point clear enough? Jesus Christ's accomplishment at Calvary was too magnificent for us to live a shallow life! We must bravely step out into deeper waters, so that we may live deeper, speak deeper, and love deeper for Him! We must choose to go deeper for the ONE who is The River, The Fire, The Eagle, and The Voice to EVERY generation.

In 2014, Phillip Baker Ministries (PBM) launched *The Daily Move!* Through a daily email, PBM began to give away a "Move," or rather, a "nugget of truth;" that would help people move into deeper waters. My sincere goal was to MOVE people using *The Daily Move*, from being a THIS to a THAT. A THIS is what you currently are and a THAT is what you desire. For example, you were shy, now you are bold, you were angry, now you are full of love, you were addicted, now you are free. Ultimately I wanted to enable these people to MOVE into deeper waters. I amassed these precious truths from 25 years of preaching God's Word, and from incredible, supernatural experiences I have had throughout my entire life. *The Daily Move* was not going to be about the *quantity* of words; but rather, it would be about the *quality* of words. Personally, I feel that there is far too much rambling in God's pulpits around the world. PBM wanted every day's "Move" to be short and sweet, but still contain power and truth that could MOVE someone's life forward into deeper waters. With the help of the Holy Spirit, *The Daily Move* has accomplished these goals. Almost every day, I receive feedback regarding a specific "Move" being delivered at just the right time to ensure deliverance and progress in someone's life situation. In *THE MOVE,* chapters 2 through 5 contain the "nuggets of truth" that I believe best represent "The Deep Life!" My heart's desire is that each "Move" will remain with you and impact you in different ways. I pray that each "Move," MOVES you!

I have provided a quick overview of what lies ahead as you journey through this book. To begin with, chapters 2 through 5 contain 100 Moves that cover topics such as Our Father, Jesus Christ, the Holy Spirit, Our Love Walk, and Faith. These chapters will surely impact your life in a powerful way. The subsequent chapters will introduce you to your Kingdom Assignment, Favor, and a God who turns things around. Additionally, I will reveal a formidable and prominent enemy of the Deep Life. There is a chapter with a strong call for us all to leave God's Churches greater than how we first found them, and finally there is a message for the next generation. Each of these chapters will contain many more Moves that will MOVE you! All in all, this book contains 222 Moves! Each one of these Moves is very special to me, because each one of them is so deeply a part of my identity. My hope is that you come to cherish each Move the way I do.

Okay, it is time to jump right in! In the previous paragraph, I mentioned that I have had some incredible supernatural experiences. These supernatural experiences shaped me in such a powerful way. In the very first chapter of *THE MOVE*, I will share some of these mind-blowing experiences with you. I truly believe that you will realize, without encounters with The Father, Jesus, and the Holy Spirit, there can be no Deep Life.

Enjoy The Journey – Phillip Baker

CHAPTER 1

SUPERNATURAL ENCOUNTERS

To begin with, it would be impossible to emphasize the need to move from the shallow to the deep, without sharing some deep encounters I have had with my Father God, my Lord Jesus, and the Holy Spirit, the last of whom has been my friend since I was 15 years old. As a matter of fact, a Deep Life cannot come into being without encounters with a Deep God! Please understand that you do not have to see Him with your eyes, audibly hear His voice, or have a vision of Heaven. In other words, an encounter with a Deep God does not require that your physical senses be involved 100%. This is because you are not simply touch, taste, smell, sight, and sound! You are a spirit being, and therefore, God is more than capable of touching you right there in your spirit. However, since God is God, He can always choose to reveal Himself to you through any one of your five senses! Finally, you may be asking yourself, "what is an encounter with the deep?"

An Encounter is an experience where God makes Himself real to you!

Moreover, the encounters I have had throughout my life are more precious to me than anything in the world. I have multiple reasons for wanting to share these encounters with you. First of all, these encounters are a part of this book so that my children, and my children's children may know how God made Himself real to me. My hope is that *THE MOVE* will inspire them to reach out to God, and move into The Deep for their own experiences. Secondly, the encounters are in this book to help you build up a supernatural expectation for the "Moves" in the upcoming chapters. Lastly, these supernatural encounters are in this book to honor and to thank my Heavenly Father for touching my life. Thank you, Father, for all the encounters of the past, and also for the ones that are still yet to come! Are you ready? Here we go!

The Bathroom Floor!

When I was seven years old, I made my way down the aisle and to the altar of Calvary Baptist Church in Cullen, Louisiana. Without a doubt in my mind, I know that I was reaching out to Jesus that day, as He was reaching out to me. As the Pastor was preaching the Gospel that day, I heard him. The Pastor gave an altar call to accept Jesus as Lord and Savior, and I raised my hand. I was the only one that day to raise my hand, and when the Pastor invited me to the front, I went up to the altar with every eye on me. To be honest, I only remember the Pastor praying over me and sitting down with my granddaddy to fill out a membership card. I wish I could tell you that the moment was deeper than that, but that is all that happened that day. However, the story did get better about a week later when I got up in the middle of the night to use the bathroom. I remember that the white porcelain heater was on and the bathroom was so warm and cozy. Do you remember those gas heaters and the days before central air and heat? Sorry, I digressed from my story! So, I sat down in the warmth of the heater and stared at the flames; and in that moment, I experienced an intense quiet. In the midst of the profound stillness, I encountered the surreal Presence of my Father. All of a sudden, spiritual truths became so clear to me! That night I know that Jesus Christ became my Lord and Savior. I firmly believe that what the Father started at the altar in Calvary Baptist Church, He finished on the bathroom floor. Thank you, Jesus, for that bathroom floor and that warm gas heater at 406 North Arkansas Street in Springhill, Louisiana! Every Deep Life begins with a salvation story!

The Camp at Caney Lake!

When I was 15, I attended Caney Lake Camp in Minden, Louisiana. There were about 70 young people in attendance that summer. This particular camp was owned by the Methodist denomination, and it was a very nice camp with cabins and a clean lake where we could swim. Everyone was having a great time, but little did we know that an encounter with the supernatural was coming our way; and it would change everything. I remember that night like it was yesterday! My friends and I were sitting on the back row, where "cool kids" always sat, as Barry Jackson, the guest speaker, walked to the pulpit. Suddenly,

Brother Jackson knelt on one knee and began to sing, and as he sang the Glory of God fell in that place. All heaven broke loose! Young people all around me were worshipping God, and youth pastors were praying for the teenagers who were falling down, right and left under the Power of God! It was like a bomb had gone off, and meanwhile my friends and I were still sitting on the back row clinging to our "cool" status with all our might. The next thing I knew, Benny Anglin, my youth pastor, sent Crystal, one of the girls, to get us off that back row. Once we were all up there in the front, Benny lined us up with me on the far end and he began to pray and lay hands on us. Every boy he laid his hands on fell to the ground weeping, and as he got closer and closer to me a strange feeling began to overtake me from the inside out. The closer he got to me, the more I began to laugh! No matter how hard I tried, I could not stop laughing. I think Pastor Benny even thought I was laughing at my weeping friends who were all lying on the ground already. When he finally laid his hands on me, I collapsed to the floor and for quite some time an uncontrollable joy poured out of me! In this supernatural encounter, the Father made Himself real to me as I was filled with the Holy Spirit and began speaking in my prayer language. It is not possible for me to fully express how much this glorious experience meant to me when I was 15, or how much it has continued to mean to me every year since. Even after all

these years, the experience is still as real to me as it was then. I know that God is real! Since that night, I have never doubted the reality of His power, and I have never been the same. Like I said earlier, when I got up from the floor I was praying in my new prayer language. There was a boy nearby, that I did not know, who made fun of me. I went to the restroom, and again a strange feeling came over me; and I had another encounter with the supernatural. In that bathroom, I began to hurt in my heart for the boy that had made fun of me. So, with my new prayer language, I began to pray for him. After a few minutes had passed, I felt peace in my heart and I went back to the sanctuary. The first thing I saw was the boy I had just prayed for, and he was falling down under the Power of God and I saw him receive his prayer language. Immediately, I knew that God had used me to pray for that boy; so that he could also have an encounter with the supernatural. As you can probably guess, I came home from Caney Lake, and life from then on was different and deeper. The experience I had with the Holy Spirit opened my eyes to the working of His Power, and I liked it so much that I have been chasing that night ever since!

The Wisdom of Solomon!

Obviously, the encounter I had at Caney Lake changed my life and set me on the right track, but there was much more to follow. Once I got home, I decided to read my Bible every night before I fell asleep; and what better place to start than at the beginning, in the book of Genesis? As time passed, I made my way through the Old Testament and found myself in 1 Kings the 3rd chapter. The memory I have of me in my room that night, reading about Solomon asking God for wisdom, is so vivid! The story caught my attention in a great way, because Solomon was a young man like me when he asked God for wisdom. In that moment, I became intently aware of the Presence of God in my room. I knew in my heart that the Father wanted me to ask for wisdom like Solomon had asked for wisdom. So, I did exactly that; I asked the Father for WISDOM! The funny part is that I did not fully know what wisdom even was, but I asked for it anyway. I firmly believed that if God gave me wisdom, then everything else in life would fall right into place. Is that not what happened in the case of Solomon? Solomon asked for wisdom and God also gave him long life, honor, and riches. From that night on, my life was never the same. For instance, the Word of God became more clear and comprehensible, stupidity became more obvious, and I began to think far more about my future, than I did about my present. In no way am I comparing my wisdom to Solomon's wisdom or to anyone else's wisdom, but I am convinced that I received a gift from Heaven that night. I received something precious that would serve to establish and propel me toward my destiny. That precious something was the Wisdom of God, and furthermore; my desire to move further into the deep intensified! Every Christian can have a WISDOM encounter, but you must get still, get quiet, and ask for WISDOM! The Father is still looking for people who will ask for that which Solomon asked!

Face to Face!

Since the Boston Celtics were playing the Lakers in the 1984 NBA finals, camp could not have come at a worse time. I did not want to go to camp! Not only did I love the Celtics, but I also could not stand the Lakers with their purple and gold jerseys. However, my youth group and all my friends were going to camp, so I was going to camp! Before I left, my mom made a comment about me being called to ministry. I remember flippantly saying (as only a teenager can, with the traditional rolling of the eyes to accompany my comment), "Jesus would have to appear to me face to face in order for that to happen." The moronic stuff we say sometimes that we don't think God hears is absolutely amazing! Little did I know how much that one flippant response would affect my camp experience, and for that matter, the rest of my life.

During that camp weekend, there was an outdoor concert with the Songwriters. My memory of this concert is as clear today, as it was then. I was sitting on a hill listening to the Songwriters sing a song that described the crucifixion of Jesus. I recall that I closed my eyes to focus in on the powerful lyrics of the crucifixion song, and unexpectedly I was caught up in a vision! I found myself walking up a hill. Once I had made it to the top of this hill, I was stunned to see The Cross of Calvary brought forward, and then dropped into a post hole that was right at my feet. Suddenly, I was face to face with Jesus Christ. There were no words spoken, because none were necessary. This moment was brief, but felt like the eternity from whence it came. The experience I had on that hill was something to be remembered! There was a face to face encounter, and my life was never the same. I knew from that point forward that ministry was what I was called to do.

In light of this face to face encounter with Jesus, I came home from camp knowing that I wanted to go to Bible school one day; and afterward step into full-time ministry. Little did I realize that this encounter on a hill in Columbus, Texas, would mean more and more to me in the years to come. Fast forward a few years, and this camp ground was purchased by Pastors Tommy and Rachel Burchfield and came to be called Discovery Camp, and the home of Texas Bible Institute. The mind-blowing part of this story is that 10 years later, to the very month, Laura and I moved to Columbus to help the Burchfield's build Texas Bible Institute! Consider this for a moment. When I was on that hill in June of 1984, the Father saw me moving to that very camp in June of 1994. Our God is an awesome God, and He lives in eternity! A great man of God once said, "God sees our past, present, and future all in one glance!"

A Spiritual Door!

After this encounter in Columbus, I decided that I wanted to see more of the supernatural! I so wanted to see Jesus, an angel, or even heaven. Throughout the years, I had heard other ministers tell their stories about seeing spiritual things with their eyes, so I felt it was my time to have those spiritual experiences. I would wager that I am not alone on this one. Every night I would pray and ask the Father to show me something. Well, one particular night, I was in my room praying along these lines, and I became keenly aware that a spiritual door had come to the foot of my bed. I knew beyond a shadow of a doubt that something was about to come through that door, and it was not going to be a good thing at all.

Truth be told, I did not physically see anything; but there was no question in my mind that I was about to encounter something or someone. I was terrified, and I am not embarrassed to admit it. Naturally, I covered my head with the sheets and began to REPENT! That night I made a commitment to the Father that I never seek visions again. I decided that I would live according to The Word, and endeavor to be led by the Holy Spirit. Furthermore, if God ever chose to give me a vision, it would be completely up to Him. Listen carefully, when you seek after the supernatural, the devil can come and attempt to deceive you. I believe that the earth is full of false religions, cults, and overall lies because demonic spirits appeared and deceived someone.

Mike, Keith, and The Crowd!

When I was in my late teen years, I had an encounter in prayer that changed everything for me. I was in my room worshipping God (probably to the 8-track by

Andre' Crouch, Live In London) and just spending time with Him, when the Holy Spirit brought back a memory from junior high. I had not thought about this particular memory since it had happened years ago. It began with me walking to school. Yes, I did walk to school, but do not feel sorry for me, because it was not that long of a walk. When I arrived on the school grounds, I saw a large crowd of people gathered together. Like a moth to the flame, I went over to see what was happening. What I saw that day deeply upset me! Keith, the kid everyone at school picked on, was in the middle of the crowd getting bullied. Keith was crying and just wanted to escape.

I experienced multiple reactions to the situation. Not only did I feel bad for Keith, I was also infuriated by what those people were doing to him; but more than that, I felt guilty for being glad it was him and not me. See, as a kid, I was picked on because I was not the most popular, smartest, or the most athletic. For a time in my life, I even stuttered. It was a very dark time in my life, because we all know how kids can be about those things. So, I definitely knew what it was like to be bullied, and I had so much sympathy for Keith that day. For those of you who can relate to this sentiment, I believe this story, and this book in general, is going to be a great blessing to you.

Getting back to the original story...I was standing there watching Keith, feeling all these different emotions, when out of nowhere Mike walked into the crowd. Let me tell you a little bit about Mike! Mike was the alpha male, and he was the greatest athlete in junior high. He was the guy with muscles where no one else had muscles in junior high school. No one EVER messed with him, and that continued to be the case even into high school. That day, Mike walked up and said something to everyone. To be honest, I do not even remember what he said; but as soon as the words had left his mouth, the crowd dispersed! Keith walked away from the whole situation relieved, and I went to class. This was the entire memory that the Holy Spirit brought back to me that night while I was in prayer.

Obviously, I knew that the Holy Spirit was endeavoring to teach me something by bringing that memory to my mind all those years later. You may be asking, "What was the lesson that I needed to learn?" Well, the Holy Spirit was showing me what my life was supposed to be, and that day I decided three things! First, **I would not be a Keith all my life!** My mind was made up that I would not be a victim, and sit around licking my emotional wounds. I decided that I would not become an offended and bitter person. Secondly, **I would never be the crowd!** I would not spend my life putting people down to make myself feel superior to others. More specifically, I would not be a bully, either by my actions or my omission to stop the actions of others. Neither would I shine a light on other people's flaws and weaknesses. In fact, I decided that I would rather be picked on, than to pick on someone else. Lastly, **I made the ultimate decision in my room that night to be a Holy Spirit-Filled Mike!** For the rest of my life, I would be the person who stood up to crowds, and stopped bullies in their tracks. My goal would now be to protect the "Keiths" of the world. Moreover, I would help these people become a "Mike," and not remain a "Keith" their entire life. I realized that the "Keiths" did not have to live their lives as captives, but with the Power of the Holy Spirit these people could be set free to become deliverers themselves! Only God knows how many young people I have told this story to before, and only He knows how many I have challenged to be a "Mike" in their world! In conclusion, do not be a bully, choose to BE A MIKE!

The Dream!

Shortly after Laura and I married, I had an encounter with the Father in a dream that impacted me tremendously. In this dream a man that I know in real life was talking to me. Laura remembers me waking her up and asking for a pen and paper to write it down. It was so powerful that I could not risk going back to sleep and forget it. I believe that these are the most supernatural words you, or I will ever hear. To this day, I know that these words came straight from heaven. I take zero credit for the words that were spoken to me in this dream, and they have permanently burned into my spirit and soul ever since.

Christ wants to make a perfect work of your life, You can make your life perfect through Christ's Work!

In the dream, the man looked at me and said, **"Overachieve!"** All my life teachers had said that I was an underachiever. Has anyone ever called you an under-achiever before? Have you ever felt like you were not living up to your full potential? I sure have! Honestly, this subject is what a large part of this book is all about. Do we want to live up to our full potential in life? Do we want to live up to our full potential In Christ?

Amazingly, in this dream I had The Father telling me to overachieve. Ever since that night, I have determined to give Him my very best. This is because I knew then, what I also know now; the Father gave us His best, and His best was JESUS! Furthermore, Jesus gave us His best, because Jesus gave us His Life!

In the following chapter, the Moves will begin to impact your life in a mighty way. They will begin to MOVE you deeper. In other words, they will begin to MOVE you towards your full potential. My heart's prayer is that each Move will MOVE you!

MOVE YOU:

From shallow to deep
From a puddle to a river
From natural to supernatural
From ordinary to extraordinary
From captive to deliverer
From customer to servant

From watcher to worshipper
From smoke to fire
From parrot to eagle
From Quoter to Declarer
From Victim to Victor
From Religion to Relationship

From a taker to a giver
From mission field to missionary
From my ways to His ways
From Keith to Mike
From death to life
From empty to overflowing
From orphans to sons
From spark to a flame
From prisoner to a prince
From negative to positive
From echo to voice
From offended to a forgiver
From knowledge to wisdom
From selfishness to love
From doubt to faith
From memories to vision
From enough to more than enough

From In Adam to In Christ
From less to more
From a mess to a message
From duty to vision
From a griper to a praiser
From distracted to focused
From apathy to passion
From Glory to Glory
From weak to strong
From fear to fearless
From sinner to saint
From a copy to an original
From comfort zone to risk
From Hell to Heaven
From needy to needed
From lazy to disciplined

From underachiever to overachiever!

In the following four chapters, you will encounter 100 Moves that best represent the Deep Life. Turn the page, if you are ready to get Moving!

CHAPTER 2

TIME TO MOVE I

Move #1 Deep or Shallow?

Psalm 42:7 says, "*deep is calling unto deep...!*" The deep in God is calling out to the deep in us. The question is, "Are we hearing it?" When you live in the shallow, your life is defined by emotions, circumstances, and the storms of life. However, living in the deep is much different. A life lived in the deep is defined by revelation, power, and purpose.

Move #2 King of Kings!

It is time for "The Kings" to wake up! You are probably asking, "Who are the 'The Kings'?" The answer is, *you* are a King! Jesus is THE KING, and you are His King in the earth. Jesus is THE PRIEST, and you are His Priest in the earth. Now is the time to rise up, and to begin to rule and reign as a King and a Priest of KING JESUS! There is a Kingdom to be built; and it is your responsibility as His King, to build it.

Move #3 A Kingdom Declaration

God put a declaration in my heart many years ago that has come to the surface every time I have felt down, intimidated, or worried. During these times, I have boldly declared, "All of Heaven is behind me. The Holy Spirit is working in me. The Angels are working for me!" I challenge you to begin making this same Kingdom Declaration, so that you will also be able to experience boldness and faith rising within you!

Move #4 Who Are You?

Abraham was a Father. Moses was a Deliverer. Elijah was a Prophet. David was a King. Peter was a Disciple. Paul was an Apostle. The question is, "What are you, other than a Believer in Jesus?" The truth is, we must know who we are, and we must know our path. Ultimately, we must know our role and place in The Kingdom of God.

Move #5 My Life Motto!

My Life's Motto is, "Aggressive Faith and a Gentle Spirit." Those few words are what I have used to guide my life, day in and day out. At the end of the day, I do not want to only have great faith and no love. On the other hand, I do not want to have great love and no faith. I want both powerful attributes operating in my life! Truly, I have not arrived yet; but I have left. By the way, "Aggressive Faith and a

Gentle Spirit" are words that perfectly describe our Savior, Jesus Christ.

Move #6 The Dream!

I had a dream during my late teen years that totally changed my life! When I awoke, I immediately wrote down the words that were spoken to me in this supernatural dream.

"Christ wants to make a perfect work of your life. You can make your life perfect through Christ's Work!"

I truly believe these words came straight from heaven, and perfectly embody the Gospel of Jesus Christ.

Move #7 Supernatural Words!

Upon my first visit to Africa, the Holy Spirit dropped the following dynamic confession into my spirit:

"Father, I trust you!
Jesus, I will follow you!
Holy Spirit, I need you!
Angels, I welcome you!
Satan, I rebuke you!"

Indeed, these are the most supernatural words that can come out of a believer's mouth. I encourage you to begin proclaiming these very words, and I promise that you will behold great changes in your daily life!

Move #8 Father, I Trust You!

You saying "Father, I trust you," means more to our Heavenly Father than saying, "I love you." The reason for this is obvious, because we can love people and not trust them. The same holds true for our relationship with God. It is one thing to love God, but trusting Him is another story altogether. The question is, "Do you *trust* the Father?" Let us all determine to grow in trusting our Heavenly Father every day.

Move #9 Jesus, I Will Follow You!

Lordship is about letting Jesus lead the way. Our hearts should cry, "Jesus, I will follow you!" We must understand that Jesus drives and we ride. Jesus is our master. In other words, Jesus is THE boss! There are so many believers who have made Jesus their Savior, but have not proceeded to living under His Lordship! Make Jesus Lord over your life today!

Move #10 Holy Spirit, I Need You!

Oh, how we need the Holy Spirit! Consider this, if Jesus relied upon the Holy Spirit, then how much more do we need the Holy Spirit?! We must have the help of the Holy Spirit to become who God has called us to be, and do what

God has called us to do! It does require humility, however, to ask for help. I challenge you to show some humility today, and tell the Holy Spirit, "I need You!" Do not wait another day. Start building a stronger relationship with the Holy Spirit today.

Move #11 Angels I Welcome You!

In the first chapter of Hebrews the following question is posed, "Are not all angels ministering spirits sent to serve those who will inherit salvation" (NIV, Hebrews 1:14)? We know that the angels assisted Jesus, the Disciples, and the early Church greatly. Of course, we are not to pray to or worship angels. We can, however, welcome their help, because we sure do need it! Let us say "Angels, I welcome you" every day, and allow the angels of God into your life circumstance!

Move #12 Satan, I Rebuke You!

We have been given authority in Christ Jesus over all the power of the enemy! All believers must understand that they are seated in heavenly places In Christ Jesus! Moreover, Satan is under our feet. We are unafraid of Satan, but he is very much afraid of the believer who understands, holds and wields their authority In Christ Jesus. We must be ready to say, "Satan, I rebuke you" with authority!

Move #13 How Sharp?

The depth of our Christianity can be judged based on our understanding of the following three truths: 1-God is our Father, 2-Jesus is our Lord, and 3-The Holy Spirit is our Friend. How strong is your revelation of God as your Father, Lord, and Friend? Truly, these incredible revelations are swords that can never be sharp enough!

Move #14 The Dangerous Prayer

Father, I want to be who you have called me to be; and my desire is to do what you have called me to do! I want to go where you call me to go, and I want to give whatever you call me to give! And one more thing, Father, I am praying this prayer because I trust you completely! In Jesus' Name, AMEN!

Move #15 He is Father, Not God!

All around the world people refer to Him as "God!" That is not the case for me, and it should not be the case for believers! He is not just our God; He is our Father. Consider this, the only way to the Father is through His only begotten Son, Jesus Christ. You must receive Jesus, and let Him introduce you to The Father.

Move #16 He is a Better Dad!

Do you have children? If the answer is "yes," think about how much you love them. What would you do for your own children? Consider the amount of love you have for your children, then multiply that love a million times over. The result of this calculation would not even be close to how much our Heavenly Father loves us. We are His children, and He loves us more than we will ever love our own children.

Move #17 He Wants it More!

The truth is that our Father wants us blessed more than we want to be blessed. The Father wants us healed more than we want to be healed. He wants revival more than we want revival. Indeed, it is The Father who grants us access to faith through The Word, in order that we may reach out and receive what He so desperately wants us to have!

Move #18 The Father's Heart!

The Heart of The Father can be clearly seen in this, "He forgives all our iniquities and heals all of our diseases" (NIV, Psalm 103:3). His heart always has been and always will be, to forgive and heal us. The question is, "What is in the heart of the Believer?" Do you desire to see people forgiven and healed? Finally, do you have a heart like your Father's?

Move #19 Jesus' Core Revelation

Have you ever wondered what was the biggest revelation Jesus carried in His heart throughout His thirty-three years of life on earth? I also asked this very question once. I encourage you to read the Gospel of John, and highlight every scripture in which Jesus refers to His Father. In the end, this will reveal the summation of Jesus' core revelation; which was that God was His Father! If this was Jesus' core revelation, then maybe it should be ours as well!

Move #20 More Than Enough!

Our Father has never just done "enough," He always does more than enough. He gave us more than enough air, water, earth, oil, gas, space, and the list goes on and on. Stop asking for enough, and start asking for more than enough! With more than enough we can be a bigger blessing to the Kingdom! He is *El Shaddai* – The God of More Than Enough!

Move #21 The Answer!

Let me be very clear about what I believe should be the solution for people, The Church, and the world. I believe that
Jesus is The Answer for every person
The Holy Spirit is The Answer for The Church
The Church is the Answer for the world.

Unfortunately, when we move away from these simple, yet profound beliefs; we end up living life in the shallow!

Move #22 THE NOT A!

Jesus is The Way, not A way! Jesus is The Truth, not A truth! Jesus is The Light, not A light! Listen, Jesus was either who He said He was, or He was just plain crazy! In the days ahead, all believers will be challenged along these very lines. We must determine ourselves not to back off "THE," and slide over into "A!"

Move #23 Marvel!

I love the word "Marvel!" This word means to be filled with surprise, wonder, and astonishment. In Acts 4:13, the Pharisees marveled at the boldness of Peter and John because they knew that these men had been with Jesus. Let us also be with Jesus, and cause the world to marvel at us.

Move #24 Billions Not Nickels!

Did you know that there are many people who are very wealthy, but they do not know it? They have unclaimed inheritance that is waiting on them to discover it is there, and belongs to them. What about believers? The wealth that believers have In Christ is immeasurable, yet most are not even aware of this reality. To put it another way, In Christ we are worth billions, but we are living off nickels!

Move #25 The Good Lion!

There is a children's book called *The Good Lion*, in which a wise man tells a little girl to get rid of her pet lion, because a tame lion is unnatural. This wise man goes on to explain that anything unnatural is not to be trusted. This idea leads me to say, "A tame believer is an unnatural believer, and anything unnatural cannot be trusted!" Be wild and free for Jesus! By the way, this children's book did not end well.

CHAPTER 3

TIME TO MOVE II

Move #26 How Did He Do It?

The idea that Jesus never sinned is incredibly difficult to wrap your brain around. How did he manage to accomplish such a thing? Maybe this will help you. Think of the worst sin imaginable, and then realize that the way you feel about that horrific sin is how Jesus felt about all sin. On the other hand, we have sin that we hate, sin that we dislike, and sin that we like. The bottom line is, we need to hate sin and love Jesus!

Move #27 Jesus' Pain

Can you imagine how difficult it was for Jesus to live 30 years, knowing who He was, and not be able to save, heal, or deliver one person? Throughout those 30 years, how many people did Jesus know or encounter that died from a sickness that He could not yet heal? It is no wonder that when Jesus began his ministry at 30, He unleashed Heaven upon earth.

Move #28 Significance!

Amazingly, Jesus stopped everything while He was hanging on the cross to settle one seemingly insignificant dilemma. John chapter 19 tells us that during His own crucifixion, Jesus gave a son a mother, and a mother a son. This is proof to us that nothing is insignificant to Jesus. You are not insignificant, and neither are your words, service, worship, thoughts, kindness, seed, or life journey! Never forget your significance to Jesus!

Move #29 Blood Then Wine!

Moses turned water into blood in the book of Exodus, and Jesus turned water into wine in the Gospel of John. For me, this perfectly illustrates the difference between the Old and New Testament. The truth is that Jesus came to give us life, and life more abundantly.

Move #30 Easy or Hard?

Perception matters! When it came to forgiveness and healing, Jesus saw one as easy and the other as easier according to Mark 2:9. How do *we* see it? Is it possible that we see forgiveness and healing, not as easy and easier, but as hard and harder? By the way, revelation changes perception.

Move #31 The Mighty Name

There is Glory and Power in The Name of Jesus! When we lift up that Name out of revelation and relationship, we release the Glory and Power that are in The Name of Jesus-and miracles happen! However, speaking the Name of Jesus out of repetition and religious ritual will amount to nothing.

Move #32 Salvation is Simple!

'Salvation,' 'The New Birth,' or being 'Born Again,' involves only two simple things. First of all, you must believe with all of your heart that God raised His only Son from the dead, and secondly, you must confess with your mouth that Jesus Christ is Lord over your life. When you do this with conviction, the greatest miracle of all takes place in you-you are Born Again.

Move #33 Christianity is Simple!

Christianity can be summed up in the following two things: obey the Great Commandment and fulfill the Great Commission! The Great Commandment is to love The Father and love your neighbor as Jesus loved the disciples. The Great Commission is to go into the world/your world and preach/live the Gospel.

Move #34 Religion vs. Christianity!

When comparing religion and Christianity, the difference is simply this: religion is "do" and Christianity is "done." The reason we do not see many miracles is because we often try to get the Father to do something that He has already done. True Christianity reaches out with faith and receives what Jesus Christ provided for us at the Cross of Calvary. Know this, we are NOT waiting on the Father; He is waiting on us.

Move #35 The Walkabout

Every time I have been to Tanzania, Africa, the plane is full of people who are on their way to take a 7-day walkabout up Mt. Kilimanjaro. Here is an idea: how about we all take a Kingdom Walkabout? In a Kingdom Walkabout, you travel with the Holy Spirit as your guide and your walkabout will last a lifetime!

Move #36 One Day!

There are people and churches that believe they do not need the Holy Spirit to live for the Kingdom of God or to build the Kingdom of God. Know this: the day will come when these people will be standing in Heaven, and the Holy Spirit will walk up and introduce Himself. I am sure that this will be one awkward moment in eternity, because they will not know what to say to the Holy Spirit. I, on the other hand, will say, "Thank You for being my best friend since I was 15 years old."

Move #37 Up, Up, and Away!

When I was kid, I was given a Superman costume. I remember that I quickly put it on, ran outside, and yelled, "Up, Up, and Away!" Sadly, nothing happened! I took off the Superman costume and never put it on again. It was not until I was filled with the Holy Spirit, that I found true power. And quite honestly, it has been, "Up, Up, and Away" ever since!

Move #38 The Promise!

Have you ever had someone make a promise to you, and then break that same promise? The Father has never done that to His children. The Father made a promise to us in the book of Acts, chapter 2. He promised to give us His Holy Spirit, but have you let Him keep that promise to you? I encourage you to ask your Heavenly Father to fill you with His Holy Spirit. Then ask the Holy Spirit to reveal Himself to you, and I promise that you will never be the same. Why? Because The Father keeps His promises!

Move #39 What is Better?

Let us look at what John 16:7 says, "But very truly I tell you, it is for your good that I am going away. Unless I go away, the Advocate will not come to you; but if I go, I will send him to you" (NIV). In other words, Jesus is saying, "It is better that the Holy Spirit be *in* you, than I be *with* you." How many Christians truly believe - or even understand that? Personally, I do not believe we, as the Body of Christ, are even scratching the surface of this revelation. I want to be someone who understands this truth!

Move #40 An Atomic Bomb!

The Holy Spirit dwells on the inside of us, and this means that the same power that raised Jesus from the dead also dwells within us! Therefore, we are capable of releasing more power than a fire cracker. We can be dynamite and impact our church. Likewise, we can be an atomic bomb and impact the world!

Move #41 Speaking in Tongues!

There is much confusion regarding the topic "Praying in Tongues!" This confusion is due to many people not knowing that there are actually four different types of "Tongues" described in the Bible. The first "Tongue" is for edification, and can be found in Jude chapter 1, verse 20. The second "Tongue" is for intercession, and can be found in Romans, chapter 8, verse 26. The "Tongue" for interpretation is seen in 1 Corinthians, chapter 12, verse 20. Finally, the "Tongue" that serves as a sign to the unbeliever can be seen in Acts, chapter 2, verse 6.

Move #42 Where Were The 380?

In 1 Corinthians, chapter 15, we learn that 500 people saw Jesus after His Resurrection! We can conclude that these 500 individuals heard first hand, or second hand that Jesus wanted them to wait in Jerusalem for the promised Holy Spirit. However, only 120 people showed up to the upper room in the book of Acts, chapter 2. What happened to the other 380 people? It is safe to say that they missed out big time!

Move #43 Want Revival?

In the 4th chapter of Acts, another great outpouring of the Holy Spirit occurred, and The Church was ushered into a *Greater Grace*. Interestingly, in the following chapter Ananias and Sapphira fell down dead after lying to the apostles. So, the question is this: what could you get away with in Acts chapter 4, that you could not get away with in Acts chapter 5? The takeaway from the story is: What you can get away with, outside of revival, you cannot get away with during revival! So...do you still want revival?

Move #44 In Every Church!

The Holy Spirit is in every church. With that being said, there is a big difference in Him being there, and Him manifesting Himself in the church service. In how many churches is the Holy Spirit standing in the corner, arms folded, waiting to be allowed to move?

Move #45 In Position?

Have you ever seen a baseball coach positioning a kid to hit the ball in a batter's box? Understand that this is what the Holy Spirit is doing with us every day! He is endeavoring to position us to receive everything the Father and Jesus have for us! Let us stop fighting the coaching of the Holy Spirit. Things go smoother, and the outcomes are better when we cooperate.

Move #46 Should You?!

Laura and I try to live by something the Holy Spirit put on my heart years ago. Honestly, we are not there yet, but we have left! We try to live by these words,

"Just because we can, does not mean we should."

I want to live a life that consists of "should and should not," and not a life full of "can and cannot."

Move #47 Lazier and Dumber!

Years ago, the Holy Spirit asked me a question that I have never forgotten. He asked me, "As you get older, are you going to get lazier and dumber, or smarter and more disciplined?" This is not an easy question! However, it has kept me moving forward.

Move #48 An Unseen Punch!

A boxer was once asked, "What punch knocked you out?" His profound response was, "The punch I did not see." This is so true, and that is why it is so important to have a close relationship with the Holy Spirit. He is able to show us the unseen punches of the enemy, and will teach us how we can avoid them.

Move #49 In The Spirit!

When you spend time with The Holy Spirit in prayer, you will begin to see the things He shows you. When you come out of that prayer time, you need to begin to declare the things you saw over and over. You will eventually see those things you have been declaring manifest! This is the purposed and desired outcome of prayer.

Move #50 Get Nudged!

Has the Holy Spirit ever nudged you to bless someone? When you obey those nudges, it releases the Holy Spirit to nudge someone to bless you. What you make happen for others, the Father will make happen for you. Have some fun today, and ask the Holy Spirit for one of those nudges. A Strong Argument

CHAPTER 4

TIME TO MOVE III

Move #51 Revelation or Distraction?

What defines your life? Is it a reflection of revelation from God's Word which the Holy Spirit has released in your life? Or rather, is your life a reflection of the distractions the enemy has placed there? Let the rest of your life be defined by revelation from God's Word. With the help of the Holy Spirit, it can be done!

Move #52 Take a Breath!

Slow down and take a breath! Please, take moment to ponder over the spiritual journey I have taken you on so far. We have been moving deeper, which involves moving closer to the Father, Jesus, and the Holy Spirit! I want to begin a new leg of this journey, which will MOVE you into the infinite love of the Father. It is this love that will grant you access to great faith; so keep moving forward, and stay the course.

Move #53 Love is a Verb!

The Love of the Father carries strong action! His love is to see us saved, delivered, healed, filled, blessed, prospered, called, and anointed. Remember, the Father wants these things for us more than we want these things for ourselves! I encourage you to seek after greater understanding of His love for you!

Move #54 Dominated!

The Father's Love can dominate you! We are called to be so dominated by His love, that we would prefer to be hurt, than to hurt someone else. Furthermore, we would rather be bullied, than bully someone else. Pursue complete domination by the Father's love.

Move #55 Who Do You Love The Most?

Consider which person on earth you love the most in your life. It is probably your mother, father, relative, pastor, coach, beloved teacher, etc. The reason you love them as much as you do, is because they first loved you. It is the same case with your Heavenly Father! We love Him, because He first loved us. Truly, when you grow in your revelation of the Father's love for you, your love for Him will also grow!

Move #56 Tanzanite!

I love Africa! The first time I traveled to Africa, I bought Laura a tanzanite stone. These stones can only be found in the hills of Mt. Kilamanjaro. The exclusive origin of these stones is the same as the Love of God. You can only find true love in The Father, and the only way to the Father is through His Only Son, Jesus Christ.

Move #57 Love Forgives!

The Love of God is forgiving! His Love destroys bitterness, offenses, grudges, and any unforgiveness you could have for anyone, regardless of what they have done. Remember, Jesus Christ forgave us, and we also can forgive others. His Love gives us the Grace and Power to forgive!

Move #58 Hurt People, Hurt People!

Have you ever wondered why children who suffer wrongs, grow up to repeat those same wrongs? The reason is this, you become who you do not forgive. When you take an offense, a seed of that sin is planted in your heart. That seed grows until one day you look in the mirror and see the person who hurt you. This revelation alone should make it evident to you that it is time to forgive.

Move #59 How Do I Know?

You may be asking, "How do I know if I have forgiven someone?" The following are ways you can know you have truly forgiven: when you can think or talk about what happened with no emotions attached, and when you no longer desire to have your "day in court" concerning what happened. If you are not quite there yet, keep praying for that person until you are.

Move #60 Love Gives!

The Love of God is giving! "For God so loved the world that He gave...!" Where there is the Love of God, there will be a generous heart. The Love of God always destroys selfishness. The Father gave us His Son. Jesus Christ gave His Life and the Holy Spirit. The Holy Spirit gives us His power. So, the question is, "are you a giver?" You are, if the Love of God is real in your life!

Move #61 Seeing Humanity!

The Love of God operating in our lives means that we are seeing people through the eyes of Jesus. Can you imagine how drastically our lives would change if we could see all of humanity through Jesus' eyes? When you spend time reading in the Gospels, you will begin to love the world and see the world the way Jesus did.

Move #62 Unconditional Love!

The Love of God is unconditional! God does not love you "if..." God does not love you "but..." The truth is, God loves you "period!" Moreover, God loves you and there will never be anything you can do about that reality. We have all experienced conditional love in our lives; and so, we know how it feels to be loved conditionally. Truth be told, it is so much better to be loved unconditionally by our Heavenly Father.

Move #63 The Quest!

In the Amplified Bible, 1 Corinthians 14:1 states, "Make the Love of God your great quest." I love the word "**Quest**." That word perfectly describes the way I feel about the Father's Love. Assuredly, growing in THAT love is the ultimate quest, the greatest challenge, and the biggest mountain you will ever try to climb!

Move #64 Someone Does Not Love You?

Amazingly, we all have someone in our life that should love us, but does not. That reality is difficult to cope with, but consider the experience of Jesus. There were so many priests that should have loved Jesus, but they did not love Him - they actually hated Him. Jesus experienced this harsh reality, and he was able to forgive and love. This means that you can also forgive and love!

Move #65 Score Keeping!

How strong is your Love Walk? Undeniably, our Love Walk is weak when we continually keep score on the actions of others. Here is an example of a *keeping score thought*, "What I do for them, they must do for me!" When your expectations are in others, you will live offended. In Ephesians chapter 6, verse 8, we can extract the following principle: What we make happen for others, the Father will make happen for us. Understand, it is up to the Father, and not up to people. So, keep your expectations in Him!

Move #66 The Rub!

How strong is your Love Walk? Listen, to have a strong Love Walk you must avoid "the rub." You are probably asking, "What is 'the rub'?" The rub is when we get offended by something someone does or says that we do not like. Typically, the offended response will be: How could they do that after all I have done for them? And ironically, the person on the other side is often saying that same thing. Again, keep your expectations In Christ Alone!

Move #67 The Blame Game!

How strong is your Love Walk? When your Love Walk is weak, you will blame The Father for things that are not His fault! Remember, it is the enemy that comes to steal, kill, and destroy. It is incredible to consider the number of people who are mad at The Father for something He did not do!

Move #68 Worship or Watching!

How strong is your Love Walk? This can be determined by looking at your worship! Are you a worshipper or a watcher? Honestly, worship is the expression of your love for God. So, when it is time for worship, are you expressing that love to God or are you just watching what is going on around you? Oh, by the way, the number one thing that watchers watch is their watch!

Move #69 More Than Slow Songs!

How strong is your Love Walk? Let us continue to examine our worship. First, people are not worshippers because they go to church. Secondly, people are not worshippers because their church plays slow songs. Finally, people are not worshippers because their church dedicates a certain amount of time in their service for worship. Once again, worship is the expression of YOUR love for God.

Move #70 Revival of Worship!

Revival, revival, and revival! I have been hearing that word in church most of my life. Do we really want to experience revival in our life and our church? Truly, we will not see revival in our life, church, or the world until we see a revival of worship! Worship opens the door to the supernatural - and revival requires the supernatural!

Move #71 Live in London!

When I was a teenager, I heard some music playing at my Aunt Lela's house that stopped me in my tracks. The eight track I stole (thank you, Aunt Lela) from her house that day was *Andre' Crouch – Live in London*! Only The Father knows how many hours I spent in my room worshipping with Andre' during my teen years. Indeed, there is no Deep Life without worship!

Move #72 Not a Suggestion!

As I was growing up, my dad would often tell me to "go mow the yard." This was not a suggestion in any way, it was a command. In the same respect, Our Father has commanded us to love Him and love people. This is called The Great Commandment, and take notice that it is not called The Great Suggestion! Life is to be lived in obedience to The Great Commandment!

Move #73 Great Commandment 2.0

Did you know that Jesus gave the Great Commandment an upgrade in the 13th chapter of the Gospel of John? He took "love your neighbor as yourself," and upgraded it to "love your neighbor as I have loved you!" Essentially, Jesus raised the standard! Please get a hold of the Great Commandment 2.0, and then impact your world!

Move #74 Never Maxed Out!

Our love for Jesus will never be maxed out! That love will continue to grow throughout eternity. Consider that reality for a moment. In a million years, our love for God will still be growing. Love God more today, than you did yesterday!

Move #75 Maxed Out!

Amazingly, the Father will never love you more than He does right now! His love for us is maxed out. That is such good news! The next time you do something great or terrible, remember that He will not love you anymore or any less than He does right now. Furthermore, your Father does not only love you, but He also likes you.

CHAPTER 5

TIME TO MOVE IV

Move #76 So Wrong!

When I was a teenager, I would often say, "I love Jesus as much as anyone else." I could not have been more wrong. I do not love Jesus as much anyone else, and neither do you! I love Jesus more than many, because I have known Him longer. Likewise, many love Jesus more than I do because they have known Him longer. We are either growing or not growing in our love for Jesus every day.

Move #77 Etch A Sketch

Do you know what happens when you shake an Etch A Sketch? Everything goes away! I challenge you to allow the Love of God to shake you today. When you let God's Love shake you, you will see regrets, condemnation, fear, worry, and sin go away! Jesus Christ died on the cross for you, so that you could be forgiven. When you accept Jesus Christ into your heart, you receive His incredible love into your heart as well.

Move #78 The Dark Ages!

During the Dark Ages, there was a great void of revelation because The Word of God was hidden away. The Word is everywhere today, however there is still a void of revelation from God's Word. Maybe this problem can be attributed to the vast amount of Bibles, teachings, and internet materials that are available nowadays. Quite possibly, it is the simple fact that society has become too familiar with the Word of God. Listen, it is not The Word we have access to, but The Word we live that truly matters.

Move #79 A Trust That Declares!

Faith is a trust in The Word, that declares! We can trust God as our Father, our Source, our Rewarder, and live an incredible life. This incredible life will allow us to be an incredible blessing to others. Let everything that comes out of our mouth be declared in the light of that trust!

Move #80 What Is Revelation?

Revelation comes from meditating God's Word; or rather, we can say that revelation comes from muttering a scripture until revelation is revealed to us. You will know when revelation comes, because a 'switch' will flip on in your soul. In the blink of an eye, you will get the revelation! Undoubtedly, when this happens you will never be the same person again! Understand that you are only one revelation away from a breakthrough and a new location in life. We need more revelation, because it is the key to dis-covering everything God has for you!

Move #81 Take Your Voice Back!

People must take their voice back from the enemy. People must also take their voice back from their personality type. Furthermore, people must get their life out of someone else's mouth! Personally, I do not want my life defined by someone's negative words. I want my life to be defined by my words, which are words that have been inspired by God's Words!

Move #82 Why Mountains Do Not Move?

Jesus told us in Mark the 11th chapter, to speak to the mountain and it would obey us; but only if we have faith! My question is, have you ever spoken to the mountain in your life, and it laughed at you? Here is the reason why that happened: the mountain does not move when we speak to it, because we do not move when God speaks to us. When we move, the mountain will also move!

Move #83 What Are Mountains?

Have you ever wondered what exactly the "mountain" was in the 11th chapter of the Gospel of Mark? Remember, Je-sus told us to speak to it, and it would obey us? Well, mountains are anything the enemy has placed in your life to hinder you. Moreover, mountains are those entities that stand between you and everything The Father has for you. Mountains are your enemies, so you must move them!

Move #84 Faith Goes!

Faith does not leave, it goes! Please, make sure that when you are leaving a city, job, or a church that you do not simply leave. Faith is always going to a new assignment, promotion, or a greater season. However, when people leave they are typically doing so because they are hurt. Being hurt is not how you want to start your next season.

Move #85 What Jesus Did!

First of all, we are not saved because of what we do. Secondly, we are not healed because of what we do. Lastly, we are not blessed because of what we do. We are saved, healed, and blessed because of what Jesus Christ DID at Calvary! It is not by "works," it is by Grace! One more thing, true Grace is followed by holiness and good works.

Move #86 The 3's of Peter!

Peter denied Jesus three times, and then told Jesus "I love you" three times. Peter preached at Pentecost, and three thousand people were born again. In the 10th chapter of Acts, Peter saw a vision three times, and simultaneously, three men knocked on his door. Why three? The Father took a bad moment and a bad number, and turned it into something special. I love GRACE!

Move #87 Desperation!

I met an older man who had seen many miracles in the
tent revivals of the 40's and 50's; so, I asked him, why
were there so many miracles back then? This man looked
at me, pointed his finger, and said, "In those days we did
not have doctors, hospitals, and medicine everywhere.
People came to the tent because they were desperate!" The
question is, are we desperate?

Move #88 Captive or Deliverer?

There are two types of people in this world. You are either
a captive or a deliverer. In other words, you are needing to
be set free or you will be used by the Holy Spirit to set
someone else free. Both the captive and deliverer possess a
specific mentality, walk, talk, and body language. Christians are called to be deliverers!

Move #89 What If?

What if I get sick? Well, what if you get healed and then
bring healing to others? What if the devil attacks me?
Well, what if you attack his kingdom and put the devil on
the run? Finally, What if I go broke? Well, what if you become blessed to be a blessing? How about we live on The
Father's side of "What If?!"

Move #90 Realm of Risk

When it comes to the deep, miracles, and the supernatural we are called to live in a realm of risk! Additionally, the Holy Spirit revealed the following unforgettable revelation to me:

"I have called you to become comfortable living in the realm of risk, or you will risk all, living in a realm of comfort."

Move #91 Pride's Favorite Letter!

Interestingly, Satan referred to himself using the letter "I" five times in the 14th chapter of Isaiah. Likewise, the prodigal son's brother used "I" three times in reference to himself in the 15th chapter of Luke. These two characters were eaten up with pride. Thus, it seems that Pride's favorite letter is "I." Let us ensure that "I" is not also our favorite letter!

Move #92 What Pride Spawns!

Never forget this! Pride is when you have something that becomes everything to you. When pride sets in, people have no choice but to live in fear. They fear they will lose what they have. Where there is fear, paranoia will soon come. They keep looking over their shoulder for the person coming for what they have. Where there is paranoia, you will create control! They will control everything so no one will take what they have.

Move #93 What I Want!

What you want will always be there, and The Father knows exactly what you want. More importantly, there is WHAT The Father wants us to want. Indeed, when you want what He wants you to want, you will end up getting what you want. Please, ask The Father what He wants you to want! This will be you taking your first step towards break-through in your life!

Move #94 The Teaching Gift!

When someone has a teaching gift from Heaven, they can take what seems too complicated and make it so simple. People will remember and understand what they said, and inevitably lives will be changed. However, when someone thinks they have the teaching gift, they too often take something so simple and make it too complicated.

Move #95 What Wisdom Never Does!

Wisdom never risks a lot for a little! Every time we have gotten into trouble we were guilty of risking a lot for a lit-tle. Every person who has gone to jail, has most likely risked a lot for a little. If you go back and look at your big-gest mistakes, you will see that risking a lot for a little lands us in trouble every time. Ask Jesus for forgiveness, and walk in more wisdom from this day forward!

Move #96 Justify and Minimize!

We all have an incredible ability to justify and minimize anything we do wrong. The result of this justification and minimization process is that we do not own our mistakes or apologize for them. Honestly, coming clean on a mistake and making things right with others requires a person to have some "deep" in them. You should try to be that type of person!

Move #97 Check Your Blind Spot?

I do not like it when a car slips into my blind spot! However, I hate that even more when it is the enemy who slips into my blind spot! How do you feel about your blind spot? Some enemies that will slip into your blind spot are: the spirit of fear who will keep you from giving, the spirit of poverty who will keep you from receiving God's best, and the spirit of religion who will keep you so caught up in the motions of Christianity that a relationship with Jesus is forgotten.

Move #98 What Vision Sees!

I once heard someone say, "vision is the art of seeing what is invisible to others." The truth is, when you see what everyone else sees, you will be bogged down in the present moment. I dare you to see what no one else sees about you. Personally, I have always seen myself going to the world with The Gospel of Jesus Christ, even when others did not! I am now living the vision, and you can do the same!

Move #99 The Fear of Failure!

You must overcome the fear of failure if you want to do what The Father has called you to do! Consider the following examples for a moment: Abraham went, Noah built, Elijah called, David fought, Peter walked, Paul obeyed, and Jesus died. The question is, what verb will follow your name when your life time is finished?

Move #100 Our Kingdom Assignment!

Jesus is The King, and we are His Kings in the earth! This means that we have been given Kingdom Authority with which to reign in this earthly domain. We also have a Kingdom Anointing, and have gained access to Kingdom Provision. Ultimately, this all means that we have a Kingdom Assignment! Your Kingdom Assignment is where "Moving Deep" takes you!

CHAPTER 6

OUR KINGDOM ASSIGNMENT

Let us begin this chapter by first taking another look at Move 100.

Move #100 Our Kingdom Assignment!

Jesus is The King, and we are His Kings in the earth! This means that we have been given Kingdom Authority with which to reign in this earthly domain. We also have a Kingdom Anointing, and have gained access to Kingdom Provision. Ultimately, this all means that we have Kingdom Assignment! Your Kingdom Assignment is where "Moving Deep" takes you!

When someone purposes in their heart to leave shallow waters behind and sets out for the deep, they immediately place themselves on a guaranteed collision course with their Kingdom Assignment! Undeniably, there is no Deep Life without being who God has called you to be, and doing what God has called you to do. The Deep

Life is a life lived with avowed purpose. However, contrary to the assumptions of a lot of people, fulfilling your Kingdom Assignment does not mean that you must become a preacher. Truly, there are more Kingdom Assignments that have nothing to do with preaching, than there are that do. So, take a deep breath and relax! This chapter is not intended to persuade you to become a Pastor, Apostle, Teacher, Evangelist, or Prophet. In the end, this chapter is focused on helping you recognize how God has called you to MOVE the Kingdom forward, and there are numerous ways to do just that. Let me first share a true story that will simplify the overall message of Kingdom Assignment. This story involves one of my favorite moments during my world travels as an evangelist. I tell this story often in churches, and I believe it will remain with you a very long time.

A few years ago, I was ministering in Vanuatu, on the island of Port Villa, with one of my heroes, Dr. Graham Baker and his lovely wife, Irene Baker. Both of whom are credited with transforming the nation of Papua New Guinea. (I would love to tell you that we are related, but unfortunately, we only share the same last name.) Anyway, I was training pastors by day, and we were holding crusades at night. We were having a great time ministering on Port Villa, and many were being saved, delivered, and healed through the incredible miracles that were taking place daily.

One afternoon, we were able to find some free time in which Dr. Graham decided that we should go visit a tiny island called Erakor. Dr. Graham felt that it would be a wonderful place to take some pictures and relax for the afternoon. Honestly, one of the best side benefits of going to the world with the Gospel of Jesus Christ, is that you get to *see* the world! Upon arriving, I discovered that Erakor was a resort with beautiful beaches, bungalows, and a nice little restaurant. This place was a paradise, and that is why so many people choose to be married on Erakor.

Interestingly, I discovered that Erakor was a mission station back in the 1800's, and this is where this story turns deep! As a matter of fact, every time I go to the world with the Gospel, Jesus always has a "moment" waiting for me. These momentous experiences are what take my life into deeper waters. My hope is that you also go on a mission trip one day, because I promise that Jesus will have something very special waiting for you there. Then, you too will have a "moment with Jesus."

As Dr. Graham and I walked around this island, my eyes sought to take in the pristine scenery of a tiny island surrounded by crystal clear water. The great palms, with their fronds swaying in the warm breeze, and the vibrant green hues of the many ferns growing beneath; as well as the ever-blooming array of tropical flowers, added the final touches to this masterpiece of landscape that was before me. The long stretches of soft, golden beaches were incredibly difficult to walk away from as we continued our survey of Erakor.

As we ventured deeper into the island foliage, we suddenly came upon an old, outdoor church that had no roof or walls. There were no chairs or pew benches, only boards to sit on for those who attended this church. There was however, a pulpit from which a minister could preach the Gospel. I found it amazing that the commercial resort preserved and carefully tended to this historic site. Apparently, the people honored the great work that had been done here for the Kingdom years ago. I took some pictures of this outdoor church and was about to continue my tour of the island when I came upon a sight that stopped me dead in my tracks. Here at my feet were two tombstones, which bore engravings that changed my life forever. The following is what the tombstones read:

In Loving Memory of Amanda Bruce, wife of the Rev. J.W. Mackenzie who died at Erakor, 30th April, 1893. After 21 years of Christian work her last words were, "I know that Jesus is mine and I am His." Blessed are the dead, which die in The Lord.

In Memory of Joseph A. who died Dec. 25th, 1875; Aged 13 months. Arthur who died Sep. 3rd 1878; Aged 19 months. Walter B. who died Feb. 12th, 1887; Aged 13 months. Beloved children of J.W. and Amanda Mackenzie.

After reading these engravings, I found myself wondering who these people who gave their life for the Gospel were? Not only that, but who were these people who saw three of their small children die on that tiny island? Where were they from, and how did they get here? What happened to J.W. Mackenzie, and how many people were born again through their ministry? What miracles did they see when they ministered there on Erakor? What was their inspiration to do mission work there in the first place? What had drawn them to this tiny island? I had so many questions standing there that day on Erakor. With a little research, I later discovered that these people were from Canada, and that they had left their homeland behind for the mission field, with no intention of ever returning. Even at this, however, I was still left with so many unanswered questions, but I found comfort in the thought that their story was recorded in Heaven. I am sure you know by now that people are forgetful, but God **never** forgets. Every person who has given their life for the Gospel of Jesus Christ has their story recorded in heaven for all eternity. In that somber moment, standing there gazing at these two tombstones, I began to smile, as I realized that one day I would get to meet Amanda Mackenzie!

Most assuredly, I will find Amanda Mackenzie in Heaven in the future! I will find out where she lives, knock on her mansion door, introduce myself to her, and ask her to please tell me her story. What do you think her reaction will be? First, Amanda will probably want to know how I know her. This is where I will tell her that I did mission work in Vanuatu, and came across her tombstone in 2014! I believe at this point we will sit down, and she will begin the tale of her incredible life. Amanda will enjoy telling me her story, and I will be so blessed and happy to hear it! However, when the story is finished something momentous will happen. Amanda will look at me and say, "Now that you have heard my story, how about you tell me yours?" Honestly, I have always been focused on building God's Kingdom; but as I stood in front of those tombstones that day, I became much more committed to fulfilling my Kingdom Assignment. Indeed, I will have a story worthy of telling Amanda Mackenzie, and anyone else in Heaven who gave their life for the Gospel of Jesus Christ!

Now, what about you? Will you have a story to share with Amanda Mackenzie? The sad truth is that most believers do not have a story worth telling. Most of them only have a salvation story. Please do not misunderstand me, because that story is extremely important! If it had not been for them asking Jesus to be Lord and Savior of their life, they would not even have the opportunity to spend eternity in Heaven. Here is something to think about though, do these believers want to spend eternity with people from all generations and every part of the world, who gave their lives for the Gospel of Jesus Christ; while all they have to share is their salvation story? These believers will only be able to recount that one glorious day in which they accepted Jesus as their Savior, and the rest of their life was defined by circumstances, hurts, bitterness, anger, regret, guilt, and just plain shallow living! Consider the following: when Amanda looks at you and asks you about your story, what story will you have to tell?

Your greatest story, the most epic account of your life, will always be in your obedience to your Kingdom Assignment. Your life's saga is your Kingdom Assignment! This chapter is designed to help you understand the importance of your Kingdom Assignment, and also to help you discover what exactly that entails. So, let us continue MOVING forward and deeper!

Move #101 We All Know!

We have all been given a great Kingdom Assignment for our lives! When we say these words out loud, we either smile from ear to ear or our heads drop down in shame. We all know whether our life is in alignment with our Kingdom Assignment or not. Furthermore, we all know if our life is moving the Kingdom forward, or not doing anything for the Kingdom at all. We all know the answers to these questions!

Move #102 Hot Pursuit!

Life is to be lived in hot pursuit of your Kingdom Assignment! We are supposed to be living in hot pursuit of discovering your Kingdom Assignment, or living in hot pursuit of fulfilling your Kingdom Assignment. Get in hot pursuit!

Move #103 He Knows!

The Holy Spirit knows your Kingdom Assignment! You will not be able to fulfill that Assignment without the Holy Spirit revealing it to you, and you must develop a deeper relationship with Him if you want Him to unveil it to you. For He is our teacher, our guide, and our friend. The Holy Spirit is there to help you say, "Yes" to Jesus and "Yes" to your Kingdom Assignment. Lastly, the Holy Spirit will also help you complete your Kingdom Assignment.

Move #104 Stir It Up!

Praying in the Spirit stirs up your Kingdom Assignment, and none of us are doing enough stirring! When we pray in our Heavenly Language, the language that came from us being baptized with the Holy Spirit, we are praying aloud the Will of God in our life! Incredibly, this dynamic language is one of the greatest gifts ever given to the believer! Let us use it more often!

Move #105 Why People Backslide!

When you lose sight of your Kingdom Assignment, your spiritual life will begin to slide backwards. Many Christians have wondered why other Christians backslide? The truth is, these backsliding believers *never discovered* their Kingdom Assignment, and then they abandoned the pursuit of it altogether. Your Kingdom Assignment will always MOVE you towards a deeper and greater relationship with Jesus.

Move #106 Presence or Circumstances?

Your Kingdom Assignment will be found in God's Presence and not in the convenience of your circumstances. Your circumstances will always tell you that now is not the right time to obey God! In His Presence, you will find the answer to every question and problem that life will present along the way. So, get in His Presence regardless of your circumstances!

Move #107 Who Will Bow?

You are either advancing towards the fulfillment of your Kingdom Assignment or you are sliding back into your circumstances. Every day, every week, and every year knees are bowing. Your circumstances will bow to your Kingdom

Assignment, OR your Assignment will bow to your circumstances. Who will bow today?

Move #108 Want Breakthrough?

When your Kingdom Assignment becomes subject to your life circumstances, your circumstances will be strengthened and God's Kingdom in the earth will be weakened. When you make your circumstances subject to your Kingdom Assignment, there will be breakthrough in your life, AND the Kingdom will be propelled forward through you! Let us move the Kingdom forward!

Move #109 There is a Bull's Eye!

Your Kingdom Assignment has a bull's-eye on it that is clearly seen by the enemy. He may not know exactly what that Assignment is, but he is more committed to you not knowing, than you are to knowing what God has called you to do with your life. This should be infuriating to you, as you realize that the enemy is more committed to your failure than you are to your success!

Move #110 Three Assignments!

Do you truly desire to leave the shallow waters behind, and set out for the deep waters beyond the horizon? To have success in The Kingdom, you must discover and walk out a Relationship Assignment, a Kingdom Assignment, and finally, a Prophetic Assignment.

Move #111 Relationship Assignment!

Your Relationship Assignment is your daily, weekly, and yearly necessity to draw close to God your Father, Jesus Your Lord, and the Holy Spirit your Friend. These relationships must increase and develop. Let us draw closer this year than we did last year.

Move #112 Kingdom Assignment!

Your Kingdom Assignment is your active part in the advancement of God's Kingdom in the earth. Your role in the Kingdom was assigned to you before you were born! Every believer has an active part to play in The Kingdom of God.

Move #113 Prophetic Assignment!

Your Prophetic Assignment is allowing God to touch your mouth, so that through your voice His Will can be manifested in the earth. Unless you declare, proclaim, and prophesy, what is in heaven will remain in heaven. Furthermore, unless you lift your voice, what hell has loosed in the earth, will remain on the loose!

Move #114 Who? It is a Clue!

Here is a clue to helping you discover your Kingdom Assignment! Who or what touches your heart? Who or what pulls on your heart strings? I can assure you that what touches your heart is different, than what touches mine. Do you feel compassion for those that are poor, hungry, lost, jailed, young, old, divorced, abused, leaders, pastors, etc? Who do you feel the most passionate about? Who do you have the most compassion for?

Move #115 What Do You Hate?

I must ask you: what is your greatest pain? Everyone has experienced something in our past that caused us great pain. Understand that with that pain came an intense hatred for what caused us that pain. No, I am not talking about hating people. We can never hate people as Christians and followers of Jesus. I am referring to a person who has been sick before, and now hates sickness. Likewise, the person who has been poor, now hates poverty. What is it that you hate? If you can narrow this down to a few things, you will have gained more clues to discovering your Kingdom Assignment.

Move #116 What's The Problem?

Many people discuss the whereabouts of the greatest problems in church and believers love to answer this question. However, the "ministry of criticism" has not been given to The Church by Jesus Christ. As a matter of fact, the problem you see so clearly in The Church is a clue to your Kingdom Assignment! So, feel free to jump right into the middle of that problem and fix it!

Move #117 Full Potential!

What does "The Church" look like at its fullest potential? Does your mind see a church full of children, the poor, the rich, or the hurting? Furthermore, do you see a church focused on prayer, The Word, discipleship, the world, or being debt free? What you see is another clue to your Kingdom Assignment!

Move #118 A Warning!

Let me give you a warning to heed as you pursue your Kingdom Assignment. Be careful not to become offended when others are not passionate about your particular Kingdom Assignment. Remember, they will have something specific that they are passionate about as well. This is why the Kingdom of God is so effective! All believers are unique, and their passions and Kingdom Assignments are as infinite as their Heavenly Father.

Move #119 Do More of It!

Look at your life and determine what part of it is being blessed by God. So many people constantly ask God to bless what they do, and that is a wonderful thing! However, here is something that is equally amazing. Find out what God is blessing in your life and do more of it! What God is blessing is a clue to your Kingdom Assignment!

Move #120 Boldness!

To be sure, everyone is bold somewhere. Personally, I am bold in the pulpit and others may be bold in a business office, classroom, hospital, street or mission field. Some may be bolder with children, seniors, prisoners, and the list goes on and on. Where your "bold" is, is a clue to your Kingdom Assignment.

Move #121 100% Guarantee!

If you knew that you could not fail, what would you do to build the Kingdom? Let us take failure completely off of the board; and therefore, eliminate fear altogether. If I gave you a 100% guarantee that you would succeed in whatever you set your hand to do, what would you choose to do? The answer to this question is another clue to your Kingdom Assignment.

Of course, you have probably noticed that I have been asking you numerous questions in this chapter. Please understand that these are questions that I do not want answers to, because the answers are between you and Jesus. Jesus' intense desire is that you find your active part in the Kingdom, and He brought this book across your path to help you accomplish that tremendous feat. His desire is that you leave behind those shallow waters, and move into the deep. In the deep you will find your Kingdom Assignment, and life with become extremely purposeful. As you make a positive difference in people's lives, your life will become more significant; because you will be propelling the Kingdom forward. I assure you that at the end of your life, you will want to know how significant you were and what type of legacy you are leaving behind. How sad it would be to know in those final moments that your life was defined by circumstances, storms, hurt, anger, and selfishness! Of course, you would prefer to graduate to Heaven with a big smile on your face, knowing what the Apostle Paul also knew in his final moments: *"I have fought a good fight, I have finished my course, and I have kept the faith"* (NIV, 1 Tim. 1:7)!

Additionally, the Apostle Paul knew that he had completed his Kingdom Assignment! At the end of his life, Paul knew his "Confidential Kingdom File" had been given one big stamp of "Mission Accomplished" across the front. Personally, I want to know that I successfully executed and carried out my life's "Plan of Action." Let us determine to have an amazing story to tell in heaven to all of those who have gone before us into Glory. Remember that Amanda Mackenzie is there in heaven waiting on you to drop by for some tea and nice long chat. I pray you find Amanda in heaven, and that you tell her how her story inspired you to say "Yes" to your Kingdom Assignment. My challenge is that you say "Yes" to your Kingdom Assignment even though you may not know what it is yet! Say "Yes" to your Kingdom Assignment and MOVE into deeper waters! I want you to say "Yes," knowing that The Father will pour out favor upon your life to help you complete your Kingdom Assignment! Say, "Yes!"

CHAPTER 7

DRENCHED
IN
FAVOR

Ultimately, when you invite Jesus into your heart, begin moving into deeper waters, and say, "Yes" to your Kingdom Assignment, the Father will drench you in FAVOR! You will definitely need the Favor of God to do what He calls you to do, go where He calls you to go, and give what He asks you to give. In summary, you will not complete your Kingdom Assignment without His Favor.

Consider this: if Jesus needed the Favor of God to fulfill His Kingdom Assignment, then how much more do we need the Favor of God to fulfill ours? We all know that Jesus was the Son of God, and that our need for Favor must be greater than the need He had for Favor while on this earth. Jesus needed favor and so do we! Furthermore, Luke 2:52 (NIV) says,

"And Jesus increased in wisdom and stature,
and in favor with God and man."

There it is. Jesus said, "Yes" to His Kingdom Assignment and the Father released favor in his life! An interesting task would be for you to go through the New Testament highlighting all the instances where Jesus found favor. Incredibly, Jesus found favor with every person who opened their house to Him, with those who let Him use their boat, and finally with those who provided financial support for His ministry. It is obvious that Jesus found favor with the man who provided accommodations for Him and the Disciples to have their last Passover Seder dinner. Jesus found favor with Joseph of Arimathea, who upon Jesus' death, offered his family's tomb for the burial place of our Savior. All these wonderful things that happened during Jesus' life on earth were a result of God's Favor being upon Him in a mighty way. In the same manner as Jesus, your Heavenly Father wants YOU to say, "Yes" to your Kingdom Assignment so you can experience the release of favor in your life too! Ready to Move towards favor?

Move #122 African Roads!

Just in case you ever decide to travel to Africa, be forewarned that African roads are treacherous! While traveling across Tanzania, there would be times where we would come off a bumpy, rocky, dirt road onto fresh tarmac and go from 20mph to 100mph! Zoom! Zoom! ZOOOOOOM! That is a picture of favor! Favor is like getting off a bumpy, dirt road where you are struggling along just hoping you will make it and hopping onto a smooth, fresh tarmac with smooth sailing.

Move #123 Escalators!

Have you seen those moving walkways at the airport? Those things are amazing! Once you step onto that moving sidewalk, you will get to wherever you need to go twice as fast! The best part is that you use half the effort in the process. That is favor! Favor will get you somewhere you need to be, twice as fast, with less exertion! Let us seek God's Favor, and work smarter not harder!

Move #124 King Tut's Museum!

When I was a teenager, I had the opportunity to go see King Tut's exhibit in a museum in Seattle, Washington. What made the day so special was that I got escorted to the front of the line. That line was the longest line this boy from Springhill, LA had ever seen! Please understand that favor will take you "to the front of the line" in every area of your life!

Move #125 Right Place, Right Time!

The Favor of God will put you in the right place at the right time with the right people. When this happens to you, great things will take place. Do you need more great things to take place in your life? Declare the Favor of God upon your life, day, job, business, and most importantly - Your Kingdom Assignment.

92 • PHILLIP BAKER

Move #126 Excited Not Depressed!

When you are drenched in favor, you will not have fear, worry, or depression in your life. How can you have a bad day when you know favor is waiting on you everywhere you go? You will wake up every morning excited and not depressed, because you know that something good is going to happen to you today!

Move #127 Easter Egg Hunts!

When you are drenched in favor your day will become an all-day Easter Egg Hunt! Do you remember Easter Egg Hunts? They were so exciting because of all the delicious and fun surprises that were inside those carefully hidden, colorful eggs. You could find candy, money, prizes, ...you get the picture! I wake up on an Easter Egg Hunt every day, because I know that God has blessings waiting for me around every corner.

Move #128 Snake Hunts!

It seems like most people live their lives on an all-day snake hunt! If you go out in the woods and look for snakes, eventually you will find one. Do not be surprised if that snake ends up biting you either! Do not be the person who expects that, "anything bad that will happen, will happen... to me." Declare favor, and then get in on the Easter Egg

Hunt instead of the snake hunt! I promise that you will have a lot more fun and lot fewer snake bites!

Move #129 You Will Need Help!

When you are drenched in favor, people will come to your aid. You will not fulfill your Kingdom Assignment without help from other people. Jesus had help, the Disciples had help, and the Apostle Paul had help. Your Assignment will require help from people. You cannot do it alone!

Move #130 Listen!

When you are drenched in favor, people will talk good about you behind your back. Listen, someone is talking good about you right now! This is because people do like you, and they also want to help you. People will *want* to be a part of what you are doing for the Kingdom. I assure you, THAT is favor!

Move #131 Take it Personal!

When you are drenched in favor, people will take your success personally. Is there someone you love so much, that you take their success personally? This would be someone that you want to succeed more than they even want to succeed! This is the way The Father feels about your life's success. The Father will place people in your life that feel that way too! Why? Because you have the Favor of God on your life!

Move #132 Exception to the Rule!

When you are drenched in favor you will become the exception to the rule. Understand that you do not have to be the rule, and someone else's path need not be your path. Just because everyone did it a certain way, does not mean you must also. Just because everyone tries and fails, guess what? You won't! The Favor of God makes you the exception to the rule!

Move #133 Favor Not Fair!

When you are drenched in favor you will leave the realm of fair behind. Fair is good, and I like to be treated fairly. However, I would rather find favor with people and circumstances. When something great happens to you, people may say, "That is not fair." At this point your response needs to be, "You are right. It's not fair! It's favor!"

Move #134 Favor Turns It!

When you are drenched in favor, you will see everything Satan has meant for evil be turned to your good by The Father. Understand that the enemy does not want you moving into deeper waters or fulfilling your Kingdom Assignment; and so he will form weapons to hinder your progress. BUT GOD! Amazingly, favor will turn whatever the enemy throws at you into something that will eventually bring about blessing in your life.

Move #135 Brings Out The Best!

When you are drenched in favor, the strengths of your personality are magnified and the weaknesses of your personality are diminished. In other words, God's Favor brings out the best in you. You will walk through life with a sparkle in your eye and a smile on your face because you are covered with favor.

Move #136 An Object Lesson!

When you are drenched in favor, you will become an object lesson of God's grace and goodness in the earth. People will see you and the favor on your life, and know that God is good! Surely, we all want people to know God is good! So, let us pursue God's Favor AT LEAST to give glory to Him and testify of His goodness!

Move #137 Check Yourself!

When you see a young person who is teachable, on time, amiable, well-mannered, hard-working, generous, sincere, full of vision, grateful, a great listener, and has right relationships etc., do you feel compelled to show them favor? Of course you do! When we have these characteristics, it causes The Father and other people to want to show us favor!

With the idea of being drenched in favor in mind, I would like to share a true story that will shed more light on why God's Favor is such a necessity for you. In 2003, after a wonderful season of running a Bible College in Texas, Laura and I launched out to start Phillip Baker Ministries. We decided to base our ministry out of Dickinson, Texas. I remember that day like it was yesterday: the U-Haul was packed and the house was empty. We were ready to hit the road, except that there was one minor problem. Despite trying on numerous occasions, we had not found a place to live in Dickinson, and our only plan was to spend the night in a hotel and begin looking for a house to rent the following day.

We were sitting on the floor of a clean, empty house with a few close friends, probably procrastinating loading up our 3 little ones to begin the journey to an unknown destination. We had just prayed when my cell phone suddenly started ringing. It was my dear friend, Pastor John Gilligan who told me something that absolutely blew my mind (and everyone in the room who had just prayed concerning this very thing)! Apparently, he had run into someone he had not seen in quite a while at the grocery store; and after exchanging pleasantries, this person mentioned that they had been given charge by the owners to watch over a house just across the street from theirs, but would no longer be able to watch/care for a house any longer. This individual went on to ask Pastor Gilligan if he knew of a family who needed a home, and could move into this 3,600-square foot home immediately? There was no rent required, and all the family would need do was pay for the utilities and maintain the yard (with the new John Deere riding lawn mower that sat in the garage). I will never forget that night, that call and neither will anyone in that room. It was God's favor in action.

Needless to say, the following day Laura and I, along with Keegan, Madisen, and Mckinley were being handed the keys to this beautiful home. Someone might be saying right now, "That is not fair!" That is absolutely correct, because it is not fair at all - it is favor! We were able to live in that house for six months, and because of it we were able to successfully birth Phillip Baker Ministries. In essence, that outpouring of favor allowed us to birth "SOMETHING" for the Kingdom. You can expect God's Favor to allow you to do the same thing!

Move #138 Something For The Kingdom!

The Favor of God always has the explicit purpose of birthing **"something"** for the Kingdom! Therefore, Christians should love God's Favor! The Father loves when we embrace our **"something"** for the Kingdom. When we do, He pours out favor on our life. What is your **"something"** for The Kingdom? As you can see, this is just another way of asking you about your Kingdom Assignment!

Move #139 Declare Favor!

By all means, you must declare favor every single day! Personally, I know that I am drenched in favor. Not only that, but my family is also drenched in favor. Likewise, my pastors, as well as my church, are drenched in favor. Now it is YOUR TURN: declare it, and look for favor every day. Also, praise God for it amid every life circumstance. Make sure that you show favor to others. Those that show favor will be shown favor, because we "reap what we sow!"

> Psalm 5:12 (KJV) says, *"For Thou, Lord, will bless the righteous; with favor will thou compass him as with a shield!"*

In conclusion, I would like to leave you with the fact that The Father loves you regardless of what choice you make regarding moving deeper, Kingdom Assignment, or being drenched in favor. The truth is, Jesus loves you unconditionally. You can never make Him love you more or less, but IF you want to experience His favor, you must MOVE deeper. Remember, when you begin moving deeper the Holy Spirit will bring you face-to-face with your Kingdom Assignment, your "something" for the Kingdom, and you *will* experience The Supernatural! Speaking of The Supernatural, in the following chapter you will read about Miracles! **The Deep is full of miracles!**

CHAPTER 8

MIRACLES IN THE DEEP

A Deep Life is a life that is full of miracles! When you begin moving into deeper waters and start pursuing your Kingdom Assignment, you will experience miracles. Truly, you will need miracles to take place on your behalf to continue progressing and being successful in your spiritual journey. It is not possible to fulfill your Assignment without miracles taking place. You may be asking, "What is a miracle anyway?" Well, here is the Oxford Living Dictionary's definition:

miracle |ˈmirikəl| **a miracle is "a surprising and welcome event that is not explicable by natural or scientific laws and is therefore considered to be the work of a divine agency."**

Now, that definition does sound rather intelligent. However, I would like to examine this word from a more simplistic, yet more profound point of view. Our Father is a miracle-working God, not a divine agency. God wants you to live with an expectation that miracles are always headed your way! Not only that, but God is also going to use you to bring about miracles in other people's lives. The catch? In order for this to occur, you MUST have a miracle mentality!

Let me begin by sharing some unforgettable principles concerning miracles. Just look at the Gospel of John, chapter 2. Clearly, Jesus performed a miracle when he turned water into wine. To put it in simpler terms than the Oxford Dictionary did, **a miracle is when God turns water into wine! A miracle is when God turns a 'this' into a 'that.' A miracle occurs when God turns something you do not want, into something that you do want! And finally, a miracle is when God turns something the devil has meant for your destruction, into something for your benefit and His Glory!**

Only the Father knows how to turn things completely around for your good. Have you ever observed the Father turn something around for you? Personally, I have seen this happen many times. The Father has turned things around for churches, families, businesses, etc., right before my very eyes! Truly, the Father loves to turn things around and shake things up! Now let us continue to explore the miraculous desires of our Father by looking into His Word and at life in general. Are you ready to MOVE towards miracles?

Move #140 Water Into Wine!

A miracle occurs when God turns "water into wine" in our lives! Notice that God did not turn dirty water into clean water, because that would have been characterized as a healing. What Jesus did was turn water into something completely different and better – wine! Is there any aspect of your life that needs to be turned into something different and better? Understand that God can and will do that for you!

Move #141 This Into That!

A miracle is when God turns a 'this' into a 'that!' What is your 'this,' and what is your 'that?' Do you have things going on in your body, family, finances, etc.? God can turn it all around! This is the year in which you will experience a Divine turn around!

Move #142 Praise God!

A miracle is when God turns something you do not want into something you do want. It would be a great idea to make a list of everything happening in your life that you do not want anymore. Then ask the Father, In Jesus' Name, to begin turning these things around according to your heart's desires that line up with His Word. When He begins this miraculous work, praise Him for each and every miracle!

Move #143 For His Glory!

A miracle is when God turns what the enemy meant for your destruction, into something for your benefit and His Glory! Has the enemy sought to kill you, steal from you, or destroy something in your life? The enemy will try to make your life a living nightmare! However, our Father can turn all of this around! The truth is that the Father can turn anything the devil has done into something that brings Him Glory and brings happiness to you!

Move #144 Sinners Into Saints!

A miracle occurs when God turns a sinner into a saint! Every person who has been born again by accepting Jesus as Lord and Savior is a walking miracle! That person was once in darkness, but has now come into the glorious light of Jesus Christ! These individuals were once lost and wandering aimlessly in this life, but now they are found and living with purpose each and every day! If you are a believer, then YOU are an absolute miracle!

Move #145 Sons and Daughters!

A miracle occurs when God turns orphans into sons and daughters. If you have accepted Jesus, you are either a son or daughter of the Most High God! You most certainly have a Father, and you most certainly belong to The Family of God. You do not have to feel alone or abandoned ever again!

Move #146 Our Will Into His Will!

Regardless of being born again through the Blood of Jesus, we still have a will that is often contrary to the Will of God. A miracle occurs when God turns our will into His Will! This occurs through spending time in The Word of God, fellowshipping with the Holy Spirit, praise and worship of Jesus, and attending church on a regular basis. When does it happen? The exact date of our will transformation may be difficult to determine, but the miracle can and will happen over time in God's Presence.

Move #147 Mourning into Dancing!

Do you have a frown that needs to be turned upside down? Life is made up of highs and lows. You cannot make it through life without having your share of hardships. Jesus even said that in this world we will have troubles. From heartache, sickness, poverty, to losing people we love, we can often be left destitute after undergoing a tragic season. Truly, only a miracle could take all that hurt and turn it into joy! *"I have told you these things, so that in me you may have peace. In this world you will have trouble. But take heart! I have overcome the world."* (John. 16:33 NIV) To everyone who is in mourning today, please ask

Jesus to perform a mighty miracle in your life. Ask Jesus to turn it around!

Move #148 Ignorance Into Wisdom!

There is so much that we do not know! When we are faced with difficult problems that need solutions, we realize our incredible lack in the "knowing" department. Have you ever tried to solve all of your own problems? Personally, I know that I do not know all the solutions and I do not have all the answers. However, I know the One Who does! Through God's infallible Word, and the helping Hand of the Holy Spirit, you can grow in wisdom. A miracle occurs when God turns OUR ignorance into HIS Wisdom!

Move #149 Blindness Into Sight!

Imagine what it would be like to suddenly not be able to read the words on this page, or see anything in general. The truth is that our natural eyes are "sharp as a hawk's," but we can be as "blind as a bat" spiritually. Have you ever been in a situation where you did not know what to do, or where to go? A miracle occurs when God opens your eyes to see a way forward when there seemed to be no way! God can open blinded natural eyes, and He can also open blinded spiritual eyes.

Move #150 Bondage Into Freedom!

When God turns bondage into freedom, it is miraculous!
So many people are in bondage to something, and sadly,
many of them are believers. Drug and alcohol addictions,
pornography addiction, entertainment addictions, etc.,
have in one way or another gotten a foothold in the lives of
believers and taken them into bondage; but God has a
miracle ready for each person who will reach out to Him!
Ask Jesus for freedom from addiction because He knows
how to set you free! Trust me, He's been setting people
free for a long time.

Move #151 Fear Into Love!

Many believe that fear is the source of all evil. However,
we know that God is love and He is the source of all good!
When God takes a *fearFULL* person and transforms them
into a *loveFULL person*, a great miracle has happened!
Understand that fear will hold you back from doing everything God has created you and called you to do. Not only
that, but fear will hold you back from loving God and people. Please, right now, ask the Father to take fear out of
your life and replace it with love.

Move #152 Weakness Into Strength!

A miracle happens when God turns your weaknesses into
strengths! This is by far my favorite miracle to witness. I
have seen God turn the shyest people into people that were

bold as lions! Additionally, I have seen God turn sick people into healthy people, who in turn founded healing ministries. Finally, I have seen God turn people that were poor into people who are now blessed to be a blessing! The enemy is infuriated when God performs these mighty miracles, because they showcase His power to take our weakness and turn it into strength!

Move #153 All Things Are Possible!

Our Miracle-Working God can turn the impossible into the possible! How many times in life have you faced an impossible situation? In those instances, you could not see the answer or the way around the problem; but your failures were more than evident. However, if we would only reach out to the Father in those times (our help in time of need), our miracle would begin to manifest; and deliverance would be sure to follow!

Move #154 A Sea Into A Road!

In the book of Exodus, the prophet Moses lifted his rod and God turned the Red Sea into a road for the Hebrew people. The Lord can do the same thing for you! When the enemy is on your heels, lift up the Name of Jesus and your faith and trust in THAT Name; and watch a road to safety appear ahead of you 'where there seemed to be no way' (Isaiah 43:16 NIV).

Move #155 The Prince of Peace!

A miracle occurs when God turns worry into peace! Every day comes with something new to worry about, but we do not have to live in the realm of worry our whole life. Regardless of your circumstances, you can live a life of peace. Jesus Christ is The Prince of Peace, and He lives in your heart. Enjoy the miracle of perpetual peace today!

Move #156 A Seed Into a Harvest!

A miracle happens when God turns a little seed into a great harvest! You may be wondering, "What kind of seed are you talking about?" Well, a seed you sow can be you doing any of the following: an act of love, giving your time and energy, rendering some type of service, donating money to a needy cause, or anything else that blesses a person's life and/or The Kingdom of God. After you have sown the seed, God multiplies your efforts and a great harvest is now underway! This is the Law of the Kingdom. When you take the first step and sow, God moves on your behalf; and you will reap a harvest of plenty!

Move #157 Lunch Into a Banquet!

In John the 6th chapter, Jesus performs a mighty miracle of multiplication by transforming a little boy's lunch into a great banquet for thousands! When you offer something to Jesus, He will take it, break it, and then miraculously multiply it to bless a multitude of people. This reality applies to your love, life, money, and time! Go ahead and put your life in the Hands of Jesus today! He will multiply *YOU*!

Move #158 From Debt to Abundance!

Have you ever considered what you could do for the Kingdom of God if you had no debt in your finances? Imagine what an immense blessing to God's work on the earth you would be if you were free from that financial burden! Surely, this is why the devil works so hard to keep Christians in debt! The Father's heart desires that His children live in abundance and freedom, so that they can truly be 'blessed to be a blessing!' A miracle occurs when God turns our debt into an abundance. If you desire to do more for the Kingdom, but have been struggling with getting out of debt, please, seek after this miracle today! Let God take your *INSUFFICIENCY* and turn it into *MORE THAN ENOUGH*!

Move #159 More Jesus and Less Religion!

The world is so full of deception, and so many have fallen prey to false doctrines, anti-Christ philosophies, humanism, etc. Sadly, even many Christians have embraced religious traditions, rituals, and rules in their "faith," rather than a real relationship with Jesus Christ! The world does not need any more religion. It is obvious that this lost and dying generation that is being shrouded in darkness needs Jesus, His Revival Power, and the restoration of The

Church as described in the Book of Acts! *Assuredly, a mighty miracle happens when God turns religion into relationship, revival, and restoration!*

Personally, I believe we are all walking miracles! Every Believer has been rescued from the Kingdom of Darkness, and transferred into the Kingdom of Light by Jesus Christ! He has resurrected all Christians from death to life. Moreover, we were all on a slippery slope headed to hell; but Jesus gave us a level pathway on which to walk that ultimately will lead to heaven! Truly, we have received more than enough from our Father, Jesus, and the Holy Spirit.

Let me remind you of Jesus' words in Matthew 10:8 *(NKJV), "Heal the sick, cleanse the lepers, raise the dead, cast out demons: Freely you have received, freely give."*

Indeed, we are not just here to receive miracles from God! We are here to be vessels full of God's power and glory, through which miracles will be performed to bring glory to Jesus Christ and add to His Kingdom. Miracles were performed by the disciples, the Apostle Paul, and many other mighty men and women of God. Just as miracles, signs and wonders followed the daily ministries of the Disciples of Jesus Christ, they should also follow us as Christians. We are to MOVE through this earth with the help of the Holy Spirit and the power of the Name of Jesus! Furthermore, we are to turn negative circumstances around in people's lives - not only for our fellow believers, but also for the unbelievers that so desperately need to be saved by the power and love of Jesus Christ!

Sadly, every religion is offering "a way to Heaven" to the unbelievers who are lost and without hope. How are we to compete with all these different religions who offer heaven and salvation? The answer is: we are not to compete! Christianity is separated from these other false religions by miracles! This is the case all over the world in churches, crusades, tent meetings, and street ministries: when miracles happen, unbelievers start believing in Jesus Christ as their Lord and Savior! Without miracles, Christianity gets mixed in with every other religion from around the world. Most certainly Jesus knew the role that miracles, signs and wonders would play in the furthering of His Kingdom on earth. In Mark the 16th chapter verses 15-18(NKJV), Jesus said,

15 And He said to them, "Go into all the world and preach the gospel to every creature. 16 He who believes and is baptized will be saved; but he who does not believe will be condemned. 17 And these signs will follow those who believe: In My name they will cast out demons; they will speak with new tongues; 18 they[a] will take up serpents; and if they drink anything deadly, it will by no means hurt them; they will lay hands on the sick, and they will recover."

It is clear that Jesus combined the preaching of the Gospel with supernatural miracles! The Father, in His infinite wisdom knew that once the unbelievers experienced His goodness and miracle-working power; they would want to surrender their lives and receive Jesus into their heart. This idea is once again expressed later in the same chapter of Mark by these words:

20 And they went out and preached everywhere, the Lord working with them and confirming the word through the accompanying signs. Amen.

I often wonder if believers are aware of the necessity of combining miracles with the preaching of The Gospel! Has the local church fooled itself into thinking that it can get the job done without miracles? The hard truth is that without miracles the church will fail in its Kingdom Assignment. Consequently, this is why every believer must leave the shallow waters behind and MOVE out into THE DEEP waters where they can encounter the Glory of God.

By now you know that everyone has a unique Kingdom Assignment, but at the same time all believers also share the same Kingdom Assignment. This assignment is to turn things around for our fellow believer and the unbeliever. We are not just a miracle. We are called to be walking, talking miracles for the benefit of others. The enemy knows that this is the case, and he has forged a weapon of mass spiritual destruction that continues to inhibit masses of Christians from ever having miracles, signs, and wonders following their daily life ministry to others. This weapon was designed to keep believers out of THE DEEP, and instead keep them comfortable in the shallow waters of life. In the following chapter we will examine one of the **greatest enemies of the Deep Life**.

CHAPTER 9

DEEP'S GREATEST ENEMY

Upon making the decision to MOVE into deeper waters, you will surely encounter many hindrances put in place by the enemy. These obstacles will seek to drive you backwards into the shallow waters once again. **The primary enemy to those believers who seek to live The Deep Life is religion.** The official definition of religion in the Oxford Dictionary is:

religion |ri'lijən| **The belief in and worship of a superhuman controlling power, especially a personal God. A particular system of faith and worship. A pursuit or interest to which someone ascribes supreme importance.**

Since the beginning of human history, religion in some form has covered every part of the earth. You cannot travel to any part of the world where the people are not worshipping something. People worship the wind, statues, animals, trees, the sun, the moon, the stars, false christs, and the list goes on and on. The most remote places on earth are populated by people who are following some set of religious rules because they want to go to heaven when they die. The reason for this is that Our Father, The Creator has placed a measure of faith in every person that causes him or her to search for Him. Of course, Satan is aware of this God-awareness and has put multiple detours and roadblocks in the way of anyone searching for their Creator. These detours and roadblocks are in the form of religious systems.

Sadly, these religious systems have crept into Christianity, but believers are all too often blinded to their existence. Of course, there are plenty of false religions and cults, but I would like to focus on systems of religion within Christianity. It is necessary to recognize how easily Christianity can become religious and that this development will inevitably produce a shallow lifestyle for the believer. Personally, I have diagnosed religious Christianity as follows:

Christianity becomes religious when the believer puts a check mark in the "went to church" box on Sundays and focuses more on systems, rituals, traditions, processes, and duty instead of developing a healthy and passionate relationship with Jesus Christ!

The following MOVES are going to highlight the ways that religion has affected our faith, and these insights will help us MOVE forward in our relationship with Jesus and His Word. Are you ready to MOVE away from religion?

Move #160 Keys to the Kingdom!

Religion takes the Keys to the Kingdom (Matthew 16:19) out of our hands and attempts to put them back in God's Hands. We have the Keys to the Kingdom. Jesus gave them to us. Heaven can only bind and loose what we bind and loose. Believers think they are waiting on God, but He is really waiting on us!

Move #161 Reach Out and Receive!

Religion endeavors to focus us on getting God to do something instead of having a revelation of what he has already done. The believer is to reach out with their faith and receive everything Jesus provided for them at Calvary. We reach out and receive salvation, healing, a blessed life, deliverance, the Holy Spirit, and the deep walk! By faith, receive!

Move #162 Do and Done!

Religion is "do", Christianity is "done"! Every religion teaches you to do this and do that, then do this and do that, and on and on it goes. Religion is all about you doing! Christianity is all about what Jesus has done and we have the privilege and honor of receiving it all *by Grace through Faith*!

Move #163 Entrapped in a System!

Religion will entrap you in a system of works instead of allowing you to thrive in God's Grace available to you through Faith. It is, by grace through faith, and then, works! There are works, but they are a by product of a living relationship with Jesus Christ!

Move #164 Brilliant But Babies!

Some of the most intelligent people in the world are extremely religious! This is because religion builds the intellect, instead of developing the spirit. Were not the Pharisees of Jesus' time the most brilliant individuals in Jewish society? And yet, the Pharisees were absolutely ignorant when Jesus sought to explain His Kingdom to them. There are plenty of individuals alive today that are the exact same way: religious intellectuals who are big spiritual babies!

Move #165 Under Their Thumb!

Religion controls those under its influence instead of releasing the believer into dominion. Let me be clear, the more religious something becomes, the more controlling it becomes. A religious spirit puts its thumb on people and keeps them down. Believers are not to be held down, but released into the dominion they have In Christ!

Move #166 Bye-Bye Holy Spirit!

There is no place for the Holy Spirit within the borders of religion. When religion takes over, it immediately seeks to expel the Holy Spirit from its territory! If you do not believe this is true, consider the period in history known as the "Dark Ages." Why was this period so dark? Well, religion ruled the roost during this era, and religion made sure that people were kept in spiritual ignorance. The Holy Spirit brings light and understanding, whereas religion brings darkness and ignorance.

Move #167 Miracles on the Sabbath!

Jesus was persecuted by religion for performing miracles on the Sabbath day and 2,000 years later miracles have been confined to the Sabbath. Christians often tell people who need prayer to come to church on Sunday, rather than praying for that person right then and there! Why does this happen? Because oftentimes there is a religious system at work in believers' actions! You must understand that miracles can and SHOULD happen any day of the week in your life and through your life.

Move #168 Play It Safe!

Religion always plays it safe, instead of operating in a realm of risk. Miracles do not happen in our comfort zone. Nothing supernatural happens in our comfort zone. Religion did not raise Lazarus from the dead, Jesus Christ risked all by moving the stone and calling Lazarus forth. He did that because He had a relationship with His Father!

Move #169 Our Position In Christ!

Religion fights to keep its position instead of releasing believers into their position In Christ. Religion will not let anyone, even Jesus mess up its position in the world. This thought was directly behind the crucifixion of Jesus. Religion fights for its position, Christianity fights for the believer to find their position In Christ!

Move #170 Signs and Wonders!

Under the many layers of religion is a Gospel preached with signs and wonders following. Do you want to see signs and wonders, miracles, and healing flow like a river? We must remove every shred of religion from our belief system. We must have a relationship with The Father, Jesus, and the Holy Spirit. We must build our life on the Word! We must reach out to the world the way the church did in the Book of Acts!

In 2015, I had the great pleasure of preaching the Gospel of Jesus Christ in Acco, Israel. Because I know that I am doing the works of Jesus, my Lord, I am always fulfilled when I see people receive Jesus as their Savior and be healed from sickness and pain in their bodies through the ministry God has entrusted to me. However, to be able to do the works of Jesus, WHERE JESUS ACTUALLY DID HIS WORKS was mind-boggling! I will forever be grateful for the opportunity to minister in Jesus' country to His brethren, the Jewish people.

Since we have been discussing religion in this chapter, understand that Jerusalem is the most religious place on earth! The largest religions in the world make their headquarters in the city of Jerusalem, and therefore it is a city that is steeped in religiosity. After Laura and I had completed our ministry engagements for the trip, we were able to spend two days in the Old City of Jerusalem. We walked around Jerusalem, the and experienced The Presence of Jesus every step of the way. Although religion is at its zenith in Jerusalem and Jesus is not at the center of much of it, His Presence is in that city in a glorious way.

Eventually, we came upon the Western Wall of Jerusalem, which is believed to be the last remnant of the Jewish Temple. Furthermore, this is the holiest site on earth for the Jewish people to pray to the God of Abraham, Isaac, and Jacob. Personally, I can affirm that the Presence of Jesus was strong in this place. Was it because of the rocks in the wall, or the religious meaning of the place?

No, I believe God's Presence is there because of the ardent prayers that have been prayed there, the shed blood of God's martyrs who died there, and the intimate and passionate praise and worship that has been offered there for millennia. With my nose pressed against that ancient wall, I joined with my Jewish brethren who stood with me then and who have stood there in the past; and I opened my mouth in prayer to the God of Abraham, Isaac, Jacob, AND PHILLIP BAKER! I prayed for a Greater Glory to come to the earth, for God's Churches to receive a Greater Revelation of Jesus Christ and His Word, and for the hearts of Believers to passionately seek after their Kingdom Assignment in Jesus' Name! I also prayed for the peace of Jerusalem, and the salvation of the Jewish people through the acceptance of their Jewish Messiah, Jesus Christ!

Indeed, experiencing a Greater Glory is what this book is all about! We must understand by now that this Greater Glory is waiting for us in the deep. We will not find any of these treasures, or have any of the marvelous mysteries revealed to us while we are wading around in shallow waters. We must go deeper to experience the richness of His Presence and Power in our life. It is there that we will discover revelation, miracles, freedom, the supernatural, and ultimately, Jesus Christ!

In conclusion, I would like to ask you a series of questions of which I do not want answers. These are questions you will know the answer to, and those answers are between you and Jesus. First of all, as you look back over your life, have you lived under religion or in relationship? Secondly, do you know more about the "motions" of Christianity than you do the "Jesus" of Christianity? And finally, have you been playing it safe – wading in shallow waters – and do you now want to set out on an adventure with the Holy Spirit who is calling you into The Deep? Whatever your answers are, understand that Jesus loves you so much, and that today is the first day of the rest of your life! Choose today to MOVE forward and MOVE deeper!

CHAPTER 10

KINGDOM PASTORS AND CHURCHES

*I would like to dedicate this chapter to
the Kingdom Pastors all over the world!*

Whether it is the best of times or the worst of times, Pastors will be there for their church. All day and every day, Pastors dedicate themselves to the people that they serve. Surely, no ministry office is on the front lines of battle more than Pastors! My life, ministry, and even this book have been made possible by the tremendous impact that Pastors have had on my life. For this reason, I will spend the rest of my life traveling to churches around the world where I can bless Pastors.

Additionally, I would like to take this opportunity to say, "Thank you" to every Pastor that has believed in and supported Phillip Baker Ministries since 2003. You know who you are, and I want you to know how truly grateful I am for the blessing that you have been to us on this journey. Although this chapter was written with the express purpose of honoring Pastors and God's Churches, it was also written to focus every believer on the role their home church must play in the discovery and fulfillment of their Kingdom Assignment.

In order to fully love the Father, Jesus, and the Holy Spirit, you must also love what is most precious to Him. Of course, there are many things that are precious to the Father, but right at the top of the list are His Churches in the earth. To truly love Jesus, you must love The Church because Jesus gave His life, poured out His Blood, and expressed the greatest passion the universe has ever seen for His Bride, The Church. To understand why this is vital to your relationship with Jesus, imagine this: What if someone walks up to me and tells me how much they love me, my wife, my ministry, BUT then they add in how much they really dislike my children. And then this person has the nerve to ask to be my friend... How do you think I will react? We will have a major problem, and regardless of how much they love me, we most certainly will NOT be friends! If you are a parent, you understand this sentiment completely. The truth of the matter is that if you truly love me, you will also love what is precious to me. In other words, to love me you must love Keegan, Madisen, and Mckinley. This idea also holds true for our relationship with Jesus. I love Jesus and I love His Churches!

I understand that you may not LIKE a church for whatever reason, but there needs to be an incredible LOVE in your heart for the church and specifically for the local church where you have been planted. When I use the term "planted," I am referring to you being right in the middle of your church serving, worshipping, giving, and building relationships with your brothers and sisters in Christ.

Additionally, I must warn you that there is no such thing as a perfect local church! Each one of them has their own flaws, and I am more aware of this fact than most people. First of all, I have been in church my entire life. My roles in the local church have varied as I have served as a youth pastor and children's pastor in the past. Secondly, since 2003 I have ministered in over 50 churches each year in the USA and the world. For these reasons and many more, I am more than aware that God's Churches are not perfect, and this has much to do with the fact that God's people are far from perfect. Thank God that He uses imperfect vessels to accomplish His Will on this earth or we would all be in trouble!

Ultimately, believers have choices to make on how they will respond to the local church. Many believe that they are called to the "ministry of criticism," but as I have said before, Jesus did not give that ministry to the church. Jesus desires for every one of His followers to get right in the middle of all the action at their local church, and serve Him and His people wholeheartedly. Every believer is called to worship, tithe, grow in The Word, build Godly relationships, and come together with other believers at their church in a powerful synergy that will impact the world with the Gospel of Jesus Christ. We are called to build the Kingdom of God on earth and make the church better and stronger for the next generation. Do you see? **It is not just about you!** There is a need to leave behind a powerful legacy for the next generation to experience. Let your ceiling be their floor! My prayer is that every believer would make decisions in their local church with the next generation in mind.

As I have said numerous times before, The Move is all about leaving shallow waters behind and pushing out into the deep. The Move is a book that is designed to prompt you to desire and seek to discover your Kingdom Assignment. In order to do any of this, however, you will desperately need to be planted in your local church. You will need the Word of God poured into your life by your Pastor/s, as well as the other ministry gifts that you may receive from during your time serving in your church. Additionally, you will have encounters with the Holy Spirit in your church that will only happen if you are faithful to be *there*. Your church will be that safe place for you and your family in the future. Do not ever forget that for you to do something bigger than yourself, you must be a part of something bigger than yourself. The local church is bigger than you, and THE Church of Jesus Christ is much bigger than you! I am very much a part of my local church and THE Church, but the question is, are you?

Are you ready to MOVE towards a greater love for God's Kingdom Pastors and Churches? Then let's go!

Move #171 We Are!

I have heard it said, "the building is not THE Church, we are!" I completely agree with this statement, but the actual building of your local church is incredibly special and is the House of God. My prayer is that you BE the Church, and find a local church that you love and respect! Allow this church to motivate you to become all that God has called you to be, and be inspired to move deeper!

Move #172 100%

What if 100% of all believers served in a church, truly worshipped in a church, tithed to their church, and supported a missionary on a foreign field? What we would be able to do in building the Kingdom of God on earth would be amazing! One day I will find the church that has 100% participation, and I hope it's yours!

Move #173 30 Minutes Late!

Interestingly, people often arrive at concerts one hour early and fill up the arena from the front to the back. However, people too often drag into church 30 minutes late, and fill up the sanctuary from the back to the front. This reality reveals so much about people's priorities! Never become too familiar or take for granted your local church.

Move #174 Wake Up!

Keith Green was a wonderful musician from the 70's who once said, "The world is asleep in the dark...The church is asleep in the light." It is time for us all to wake up! We can all be more alert to the fact that there is a Kingdom to build. Jesus is coming back soon and He is not wanting to find churches waiting around to be rescued by the rapture.

Move #175 Revival of Expectation!

The Holy Spirit once spoke the following words to my heart: "There must be Revival of Expectation before there can be a Revival of Glory and Miracles." If you read through the Gospels and look for the effects of expectation on the ministry of Jesus, you will realize the great importance of expectation. When we come to church expecting the Holy Spirit to move, He does!

Move #176 Revival of Compassion!

The Body of Christ has become so numb to the pain of its members. It is time time for a Revival of Compassion. You may be wondering, "What is compassion?" Simply put, compassion is YOUR pain in MY heart. Many Christians cannot concern themselves with the pain of others, because they are dealing with their own pain. Nonetheless, reach out to others and in the reaching out, you will receive healing yourself.

Move #177 Set Apart!

Sanctification is a word that is not preached too often these days. The word sanctification means to be set apart for a holy purpose. Christians are to be sanctified, their churches are to be sanctified, and the altars in those churches are to be sanctified! Revival is on the other side of sanctification.

Move #178 The Altar!

Many years ago I received a prophetic word for a specific church; however, I believe this word is for every church. The prophetic word is as follows: "Honor the altar, and God will honor the church. Exalt the altar and God will exalt the church. Fill the altar and God will fill the church."

Move #179 Get Things Right!

Religion has stolen our altars away from us! For the most part, altars are not used in churches and people will sit as far away from them as possible. This may be because sitting too close to the altar may reveal they have something wrong in their lives. Newsflash – Everyone knows there is something wrong with them, because no one is perfect! We do not go to the altar just because something is wrong, we can go to the altar to get things *more right* in our lives.

Move #180 Revival In Our Altars!

All my life I have been hearing about revival. Truly, we all want revival in the chairs, in the lobby, in the parking lot, and in our cities! However, we will not see revival in any of these places until we see it in the altar of our church. When the altar is filled with the Glory of God, we will see our churches and cities filled with REVIVAL!

Move #181 Both 100%!

I have been training leaders since 1994, and holding leadership seminars in churches since 2003. I always begin with and build upon this thought, "The anointing builds The Kingdom and LEADERSHIP builds The Church!" Do not mistake what I am saying, because we do not need 50% anointing and 50% leadership! We can have 100% anointing and 100% leadership in our churches.

Move #182 Light and Heavy!

There are churches that are anointing heavy and leadership light, and there are churches that are anointing light and leadership heavy. However, churches do not have to choose between these two extremes. Each church has the ability to be heavy in the anointing and heavy in leadership! Choose to have both in your local church.

Move #183 Hand on the Plow!

What was Elisha doing when Elijah called him to his side? He had his hands on the plow! Elisha was not sitting under a tree waiting for the Prophet Elijah to stop by, and ask him to join the ministry. So many people want a dramatic calling! What those people need to do is get busy in their local church, and then the calling will come their way. Put your hand to the plow!

Move #184 Your Active Place!

Most believers believe that their *seat* is their *place* in the local church! I could care less where any of us sit in the church. Where is your active place in the local church? That is what matters! You are not called to sit in a chair, you are called to have the anointing sit upon you!

Move #185 Insignificance!

It would seem to most, that people who do not tithe do not love Jesus or the Kingdom. However, I have found that most people do not tithe because they feel what they have to give is insignificant. They ask themselves, "What good would this small amount do, and what different would it make?" Does this sound familiar to you? When you see what you have to give as insignificant, you will not give it. Remember, it is not just what you give, but who's hands you put it in that matters. Jesus can take it, multiply it, and impact the world with your offering.

Move #186 My Tithing Rant!

I tithe because I get to, but not because I have to! I do not tithe because I am afraid of what will happen if I don't, but I tithe because I know what will happen when I do. If tithing under the law brought blessing to the people in the Old Testament, how much more blessing will tithing under grace bring you today? The Father did not ask for an amount, but He did ask for a percentage. Why? He asked for The Kingdom, and He asked so you could live a blessed life.

Move #187 Giving Dreams!

Do you want to be one of the biggest tithers, or do you want to be one of the smallest tithers in the church? Do you want to provide scholarships for young people to attend Bible College? Do you want to support missionaries to preach the Gospel of Jesus Christ around the world? What are your giving dreams and goals? The Father wants you blessed to be a blessing more than you want to be blessed to be a blessing!

Move #188 The Church Moves Forward!

For the last 2,000 years, great men and women of God have lived and died. So many of my heroes in the faith have graduated to Heaven, and this includes many friends who were pastors that have been promoted to their eternal rest in paradise. The truth is, people come and go, but the church keeps on moving forward. The church was here before us and it will be here after us. My prayer is that we all leave our local church better than how we found it!

In conclusion, let me give you one more thought and a challenge for you to move forward with. Do you believe that The Church should be a reflection of heaven? I believe that, and I believe you do too! Well, when you read scriptures about Heaven, or when you take a close look at the what the book of Revelation says about Heaven, you will observe two things happening in heaven all the time. The people in heaven are worshipping and serving! We are going to be doing those two things more than anything else in Heaven one day. Let me pose a wonderful question for your consideration. If worshipping and serving dominates the activity in Heaven, should not worshipping and serving also dominate the activity in our churches? Absolutely! Remember that Jesus told us in Matthew 6:10 (NIV) to pray that,

"Your Kingdom come, Your Will be done,
On earth as it is in Heaven."

Lastly, to all the pastors out there who are serving God's people by sowing the Word of God into hearts and stirring people to discover their Kingdom Assignment; I would like to say, "Thank you for all that you do for Jesus!" To all of you who have been blessed with a pastor; continue to love them, pray for them, encourage them, bless them, protect them, and never take them for granted. And for all of you who do not yet have a pastor, ask the Holy Spirit to lead you to a pastor that will love you, believe in you, give you the Word of God, and inspire you to MOVE deeper!

CHAPTER 11

For The Next Generation

**Are you between the ages of 13-25?
This chapter is for you! For those that are
younger or older, you are not banned.
I just have some things on my heart for
the young people!**

For those that have made it this far in the book,
I hope you have enjoyed it. More so, I hope it has
MOVED you to live more of a Deeper Life. Being
young, you have such an opportunity to begin in the
right direction. Sad to say, that is not most people's
story. Many people, let's say people like your family,
did not become a believer until later in life. I'm sure if
they could go back, they would make some different
decisions. They more than likely have regrets. Guess
what?! You are young; you can make good decisions
and live a life with no regrets! Did you hear what I just

said? YOU CAN LIVE A LIFE WITH NO REGRETS! It is possible! I am living proof. By no means am I saying I have been perfect – no one is, except Jesus! What I am saying is that as a teenager I endeavored to live my life for God, following Jesus' lead to MOVE deeper! What was the result? I am the happiest evangelist you know! I love my life! I love my wife! I love my kids! I love waking up in the morning! I am blessed to be a blessing! You do not know one adult who is happier than me! I have a great life and so can you! BUT you will have to MOVE out of shallow waters and go deeper!

For many years, I directed a Bible school for young people ages 17-25! During those years, I would tell that age group that I believed every young person should go to Bible school somewhere for at least a year after they graduated high school. This did not mean that I thought every one of them was called into ministry! I believed – and still do believe – that taking a year off from what you want to do with your life and wholeheartedly dedicating it to moving into deeper waters with Jesus is one of the greatest investments you will ever make. I would go on to tell them that having a strong foundation in the Word of God and being able to hear the Voice of the Holy Spirit as a young person would help them answer the three most

important questions a person will ever have to ask or
answer for their life:

Who will YOU serve?
What will be YOUR career?
Who will YOU marry?

How many young people have gotten those
three questions wrong? What if you get those questions wrong? But wait! What if you get them RIGHT?!
I want you to get them right! That's the reason I wrote
this book! I wrote it for all people – seasoned veterans
of the faith who are persevering in their walk with
God, young people just starting out on their journey in
life... I wrote this book for my children and their children! I wrote this book to help YOU get life right!

Before we get back to moving, I want to share
an encounter I had as a teenager that is not in chapter
1. As a teenager, there were certain ministers that impacted my life and they all had something in common.
What they had in common irritated me. They all had
really rough testimonies. They grew up and got involved in a lot of sin. You name it, they did it. Eventually they all hit rock bottom, decided to give their
heart to Jesus, and then devoted the rest of their lives
to serving God in ministry. As a matter of fact, it
seemed like every minister I knew when I was grow-

ing up had that testimony! On the one hand, I was happy for them getting their lives on track, but on the other hand, I was wondering if I was going to have to go backslide in order to be in ministry!? I know this sounds crazy, but I am just being honest with you about how I felt when I was a teenager. I didn't think this was fair. I didn't have a "rough" testimony. I was in church, in youth group, serving God, doing right, and wanting to be in ministry myself. I was also always griping to God about it. Every time a minister shared his testimony and it began to go down this same road, I would say to myself (and to God), "Here we go again." Then one day – I will never forget it – Jesus spoke to my heart about my griping and complaining. He said,

"Stop complaining about these ministers and become a minister that can stand up in front of young people one day and tell them 'its possible to live for God and do things right because I did it!"

Message received loud and clear! No more griping, no more complaining! In that moment, I decided to live right so that one day I could tell you that if I could do it, so can you! You can do it! You can live right! You do not have to waste your life drinking alcohol, smoking, doing drugs... You do not have to sleep around. You do not have to be rebellious to your parents and authorities. You can make Jesus the Lord of your life. You can know the Word. You can be led by the Holy Spirit. You can have a testimony that you were saved FROM a sinful life instead of saved OUT of a sinful life! You do not have to be just another shallow young person wasting their life, talents, and destiny! You can be the exception to the rule. You can be DEEP!

Are you ready to get back to MOVING? Here we go!

Move #189 Who Will You Serve?

Who will you serve? One day, you will leave your parents home, move out on your own, and then everyone will see who you will serve with your life. When no one is there to wake you up on Sunday morning, or encourage you to get into the Word and spending time in prayer, THAT is when we will know! That is when YOU will truly know who you are serving!

Move #190 What Will Be Your Career?

What will be your career? How many people have a job that they hate? You probably know some. They wake up every morning and go to work because they have to, not because they want to. This doesn't have to be YOU! God has a plan for your life! Discover it young! Life is better that way, and you won't wake up in 10 years regretting what you are doing with your life!

Move #191 Who Will You Marry?

Who will you marry? Marry God's person for you, and you will have heaven on earth! Marry the enemy's person for you, and you will have hell on earth. You definitely want to get this one right! You know too many people who have a bad marriage. You do not want to be one of them! Start praying for the person God has for you NOW!

Move #192 Take Aim!

The family you came from is not as important as the one you will have! Begin now to prepare yourself to be a great husband, wife, dad, or mom! Only marry someone who feels about your future family as strongly as you do. How do you feel about your future family? You might want to put some thought into that. *Aim at nothing and you will hit nothing!* Make your Aim matter!

Move #193 What Is Success?

Here are three things to know about success: 1. Most of the time success is preceded by failure. 2. Success is not an accident. 3. Success, ultimately, is being who God has called you to be and doing what God has called you to do! Fulfilling His Will is the apex of success.

Move #194 Youth Group Christians!

Are you a teenager? Are you involved in your church's youth group? Here's another question: Are you just a youth group Christian? A youth group Christian is a teen that graduates high school and youth group and then disappears from the church. They backslide as soon as they get out of youth group and away from their parents. Be the exception to this rule as well – there is enough rule.

Move #195 Pay The Price!

People want to be called, they want to arrive, they want to be on top, they want to be famous, they want to be the best, they want to have the great anointing, and the list goes on and on. People want the privilege, but do they want to pay the price? Having the privilege means paying the price. God's call is free, but it is not cheap!

Move #196 Get In The Funnel!

Paul Troquille, a dear friend of mine, once gave me some incredible advice. He told me to "get in the funnel!" Ministry is like a funnel. We start off on the big end, it doesn't matter where, just find a place to serve. As time goes by, we will work our way down to the small end or that *exact place* in ministry where God wants us to be and where we are most useful to the Kingdom!

Move #197 Elevators!

Friends are like elevators – they either take you up or they drop you down. The fool believes his Kingdom friends are his enemies and his true enemies are his friends. Ask God to show you the difference! Don't be a fool. The rest of your life depends on it!

Move #198 Booby Traps?

The Parable of the Two Sons in the book of Luke, chapter 15 gives us the two booby traps the devil sets up for us. One son fell into the trap of sin, while the other son fell into the trap of pride. Every believer leans one direction or the other. What sin do you lean more towards – sin or pride? The Good News is that Jesus is the answer for both!

Move #199 Pride Makes A Mess!

It was not sinful people that murdered, Jesus Christ. It was people that were filled with pride. Yes, I know, pride IS a sin, BUT it is also the foundation of nearly every other sin! Pride is mean! Pride destroys families, churches, and nations! Always remember that it was Satan's *pride* that got us into all this mess! Don't let YOUR pride make another mess!

Move #200 Pride's Favorite Phrase

Pride's favorite phrase is, "I know." Do you know people you can never tell anything because "they know"? When you do try to help them, they respond with, "I know". How can you help someone like that? Let's get rid of our "I know" and just say, "Thank you so much!"

Move #201 Ask Or Expect?

It takes humility to ask for something you need. When pride has a grip in a person's life, they do not ask – they can NOT ask – because they just expect to have everything given to them without any work on their own part! When they don't get what they expect, they get angry. When it comes to praying to the Father, are you faithfully asking or pride-fully expecting?

Move #202 Have No Choice!

Satan and his kingdom know how to get you into a position where you must make the wrong choices because you feel like you have no choice! We ALWAYS have a choice. We can ALWAYS do the right thing. Do not let Satan trick you! No matter where you are – no matter who you are with – you can make the right choice! Never forget that!

Move #203 So Tricky!

No one is addicted to sticking a butter knife into an electrical socket. Why? Because it has IMMEDIATE CONSEQUENCES! However, sin is so tricky because it is a matter of delayed consequences! That's just what happened to Adam the moment Eve took a bite of that forbidden fruit and didn't immediately die... but we have been suffering for it ever since! People have a habit of sinning and thinking they "got away with it." BUT we don't get away with anything! Sin has DELAYED CONSEQUENCES!

Move #204 Fear Of Failure

Here are some warning signs to look out for if the fear of failure has crept into your life. People who are fearful of failing walk through life saying the following, "I don't want to...", "I don't care...", "I didn't even try..." Rebuke fear every day! Live a fearless life! All things are possible in Christ Jesus!

Move #205 Boiling Water!

Did you know you cannot see yourself in boiling water? Similarly, you cannot see clearly, think clearly, and act clearly when you are angry. Calm down! Get in the Presence of God and see, think, and THEN act. Great things will happen if you trust God and give Him control of your emotions!

Move #206 Climb A Tree

In Luke 19, we meet a man named Zacchaeus who would have never had his life forever changed if he had not climbed a tree and gotten out on a limb! This year, do things you have never done – climb a tree and get out on some limbs! If you are asking me what tree you should climb or what changes you should make in your life, don't because your tree and my tree are not the same tree! Instead, ask the Holy Spirit what limbs you should get out on and you will experience a turnaround in your life!

Move #207 Caney Lake

As a teenager, one night I was spending time with God at Caney Lake in Minden, Louisiana. That night, the Glory of the Lord fell and I was filled with the Holy Spirit, received my prayer language, and was called into ministry! My heart is that every believer could experience an outpouring like that! Your life will never be the same again! Ask the Father for an outpouring in your life. Come on in! The Deep is incredible!

Move #208 Manners!

Do you have manners? Manners are the building blocks of our respect for authority. Without these blocks, young people grow up dysfunctional in the realm of authority and it spills over into their relationship with the Father. Be a young person who says, "Please", "Thank you", "You're welcome", "Yes sir", "Yes ma'am", "Excuse me", and who believes that gentlemen should open doors for ladies!

Move #209 Enjoy The Journey!

Do you have a dream that you are passionate about? Something that you think about every day and are working towards seeing come to pass? Make sure that in your pursuit of that dream, you are enjoying the journey! Be just as happy on the way as you are when you arrive!

Move #210 Dream Big!

The Lord once spoke to my heart that people's "dreamers" were broken! I'm not talking about the dreams we have at night – I mean the dreams, desires, and hopes of our hearts! The Father created us to dream! We are at our best when we are going after our dreams with His help! Dream BIG today!

Move #211 Shut Down!

When our "dreamer" is broken, three things shut down and become weak in our lives. If you are not dreaming about being, doing, getting, going, or giving, your faith, stewardship and giving will all be affected! When your "dreamer" is operating on all 8 cylinders, your faith, stewardship, and giving will soar! Dream BIG today!

Move #212 Giving Dreams!

The Father doesn't mind you dreaming about getting or going, as long as you are also dreaming about giving! What are your giving dreams? What do you want to do for the Kingdom? Put the Kingdom first and you will see your dreams come to pass.

Move #213 Eagle Or Parrot?

When a young person is Deep, they will be an eagle and not a parrot! Eagles fly high, soar far, dive fast, and are respected everywhere in the world. A parrot is pretty, but people like to keep parrots as pets in cages because they only say what they are taught to say! You do not want to spend your life swinging in a cage asking for crackers!

Move #214 Voice Or Echo?

When a young person is Deep, they will be a voice and not an echo! How many young people do you know who only say something or stand up for something after someone else has already said it or done it first? They are just echoes! God hasn't called you to be an echo! He's called you to be a VOICE to your generation!

Move #215 River Or Puddle?

When a young person is Deep, they will be a river and not a puddle! You do not want to be a puddle – puddle's stink, stagnate, and attract mosquitoes! God has called you to be a river that flows, carries life, and brings life to every place it goes!

Move #216 Puddle Christianity!

How do you know a "puddle" from a "river"? You know a puddle young person when they only go to church because their parents make them, their friends are there, or someone they are attracted to is there! Take a close look at your friends. How many of them are puddles? Are *you* a puddle?! The fact that you are reading this book tells me that you are not... and if you were a puddle before, you don't want to be anymore! Stay Deep and Go Deeper!

Move #217 No Matter What?

This is how a young person can know just how deep or shallow they really are. What if tomorrow your church disappeared, your parents were gone, and your youth group friends left you... would you still serve God? Would you find another church on your own? Would you continue to Move Deeper? We all have to get to the place where we determine for ourselves that we will serve God NO MATTER WHAT anyone else does or says – and that there is nothing the devil can do about it!

Move #218 Your Best Or Worst?

There is no Deep Life without a love for God's Word! God's Word will always bring out the best in you, while your circumstances will always bring out the worst in you. God's Word will keep you in the realm of vision, while your circumstances will entrap you in your memories.

Move #219 Here Is Why

Why should a person sell out to Jesus Christ? First and foremost: YOU DO NOT WANT TO GO TO HELL! YOU WANT TO GO TO HEAVEN! And just as importantly, you absolutely want to live your life as an example to the next generation so they too don't go to hell. Finally, you should sell out to Jesus Christ because He sold out for you! Jesus loves you and gave His Life for YOU!

Move #220 Impossible Without

Many people give their heart to Jesus, but it is another thing entirely to give up our lives to Jesus! I want you to know it is IMPOSSIBLE to do without the help of the Holy Spirit. There is NO Deep Life without the Holy Spirit. He is here to guide you, teach you, challenge you, inspire you, correct you, encourage you, empower you, help you, and love you — all at the same time and as only He can do! Get the picture? There is No Deep Life without the Holy Spirit!

Move #221 Uncomfortable Silence

How well do you deal with silence? Many young people today cannot go to sleep unless there is music playing or their TV is on! What does this mean? When you are living in the shallow, silence becomes very uncomfortable. Why? Because in the silence you have to deal with who you really are without any distractions — and many people do not like being confronted with who they are! Again, how well do YOU deal with silence? It says a lot about whether you are shallow or deep...

Have you been told the truth? What are you going to do? Truth demands a response! Are you going to MOVE Deep? Are you going to be the exception or the rule? Are you going to be supernatural or natural? Are you going to be a captive or a deliverer? Are you going to make Jesus and His Kingdom FIRST in your heart?

The desire of my heart is that one day, you will be in your 30s, 40s, and beyond and will be living such a blessed life! You will be happily married, with great kids and a career that you love. You will be a humongous blessing to The Kingdom, your local church, and your pastor. I pray that every night when you lay your head down on the pillow, you won't have any regrets, but instead will only have peace! One day, I want you to be so glad that when you were a young person, you made a decision to make Jesus your Lord, by putting His Word and His Kingdom first in your life and spending the rest of your life MOVING DEEPER! And in those last moments of your life, I want you to KNOW in your heart that you pursued and completed Your Kingdom Assignment. You can do it! You MUST do it, because very soon you will not be the next generation... you will be THE GENERA-TION passing the torch on to the next generation! Leave them a stronger Kingdom than the Kingdom that was left to you!

CHAPTER 12

THE CHALLENGE

Will You Say "Yes"?

It is time to bring this book to a close. I want to give you a challenge and then finish this book with MOVE 222!

Truth has a ring. Truth has a sound. Have you heard that ring, that sound? Do you believe that I have told you the truth? If so, truth demands a response! When hearing truth, you must either say, "Yes" or "No". By not responding, you are just voicing a silent "No"! Take a moment before you put this book down and say, "YES"!

Say "YES" to:

- **The Father!** He not only *loves* you, but He *likes* you too!
- **Jesus Christ!** He gave His life for you so you could have a life!
- **The Holy Spirit!** He is here with you and in you everyday to help!

- **The Word of God!** The Word will show you The Way!
- **Prayer!** Enjoy precious time with Him!
- **Supernatural encounters!** Your life will never be the same.
- **The Love of God!** You will be able to worship God and love people!
- **Living by faith!** You can change your world by believing and declaring!
- **Your Kingdom Assignment!** Live life ON PURPOSE, FOR A PURPOSE!
- **Favor!** You will need it to finish your race!
- **Miracles!** You will need The Father to turn things around!
- **The Church and The Local Church!** They are the Answer for the world.
- **The Next Generation!** It is all about them!
- **The DEEP!** Congratulations on choosing relationship over religion!

Move 222 Father, Lord, and Friend!

You and I will arrive in heaven one day! We will run to the Throne Room, jump into God's lap, look straight into His loving eyes and say, "My Father." We will then hop down and kneel before Jesus and say, "My Lord." Then we will see the Holy Spirit standing nearby and we will run over to Him, give Him a huge hug that lifts Him off the floor and say, "My Friend!" *We will be able to do these things because many years earlier we said, "YES" to the DEEP!*

go deep!
Phillip Baker

Contact Information and Resources

To book Phillip Baker
for meetings, revivals, and seminars, contact PBM at
info@phillipbaker.org

Phillip Baker Ministries
P.O. Box 1708
Dickinson, TX 77539
www.phillipbaker.org

The PBM App
Search **Phillip Baker Ministries** in your App store.
On the App, you will find our itinerary, leadership blogs,
audio messages from recent events in God's Churches, and opportunities to donate and partner with PBM!

The Daily Move
Sign up for our FREE daily email on the website or App.
The Daily Move takes 15 seconds to sign up, 10 seconds to read,
but, will stay with you, MOVE you, all day! You have only experienced 222 of the 730 Moves that you will get by signing up.

REFERENCES

Markham, Beryl, *The Good Lion.* Adapted and Illustrated by Don Brown, HMH Books for Young Readers; First edition. 2005

Oxford Dictionary of English. Oxford University Press, 2010

Jerusalem, Israel
Gonzales, Mario Albert. Western Wall. 2016 Gift of the Photographer

Erakor Island, Vanuatu
Baker, Phillip. 2015 Grave site.

Dickinson, Texas
Laura Baker. 2018 Promo Picture.